VODKA

Edible

Series Editor: Andrew F. Smith

EDIBLE is a revolutionary series of books dedicated to food and drink that explores the rich history of cuisine. Each book reveals the global history and culture of one type of food or beverage.

Already published

Apple Erika Janik · *Banana* Lorna Piatti-Farnell
Barbecue Jonathan Deutsch and Megan J. Elias · *Beef* Lorna Piatti-Farnell
Beer Gavin D. Smith · *Berries* Heather Arndt Anderson
Brandy Becky Sue Epstein · *Bread* William Rubel · *Cake* Nicola Humble
Caviar Nichola Fletcher · *Champagne* Becky Sue Epstein
Cheese Andrew Dalby · *Chillies* Heather Arndt Anderson
Chocolate Sarah Moss and Alexander Badenoch
Cocktails Joseph M. Carlin · *Corn* Michael Owen Jones
Curry Colleen Taylor Sen · *Dates* Nawal Nasrallah
Doughnut Heather Delancey Hunwick · *Dumplings* Barbara Gallani
Edible Flowers Constance L. Kirker and Mary Newman
Eggs Diane Toops · *Fats* Michelle Phillipov
Figs David C. Sutton · *Game* Paula Young Lee
Gin Lesley Jacobs Solmonson · *Hamburger* Andrew F. Smith
Herbs Gary Allen · *Herring* Kathy Hunt · *Honey* Lucy M. Long
Hot Dog Bruce Kraig · *Ice Cream* Laura B. Weiss · *Lamb* Brian Yarvin
Lemon Toby Sonneman · *Lobster* Elisabeth Townsend
Melon Sylvia Lovegren · *Milk* Hannah Velten · *Moonshine* Kevin R. Kosar
Mushroom Cynthia D. Bertelsen · *Nuts* Ken Albala · *Offal* Nina Edwards
Olive Fabrizia Lanza · *Onions and Garlic* Martha Jay
Oranges Clarissa Hyman · *Oyster* Carolyn Tillie · *Pancake* Ken Albala
Pasta and Noodles Kantha Shelke · *Pickles* Jan Davison · *Pie* Janet Clarkson
Pineapple Kaori O'Connor · *Pizza* Carol Helstosky
Pomegranate Damien Stone · *Pork* Katharine M. Rogers
Potato Andrew F. Smith · *Pudding* Jeri Quinzio · *Rice* Renee Marton
Rum Richard Foss · *Salad* Judith Weinraub · *Salmon* Nicolaas Mink
Sandwich Bee Wilson · *Sauces* Maryann Tebben · *Sausage* Gary Allen
Seaweed Kaori O'Connor · *Shrimp* Yvette Florio Lane
Soup Janet Clarkson · *Spices* Fred Czarra · *Sugar* Andrew F. Smith
Sweets and Candy Laura Mason · *Tea* Helen Saberi · *Tequila* Ian Williams
Truffle Zachary Nowak · *Vodka* Patricia Herlihy · *Water* Ian Miller
Whiskey Kevin R. Kosar · *Wine* Marc Millon

Vodka

A Global History

Patricia Herlihy

REAKTION BOOKS

*To my children, Maurice, Christopher, David, Felix,
Gregory and Irene Herlihy, and to their families*

Published by Reaktion Books Ltd
Unit 32, Waterside
44–48 Wharf Road
London N1 7UX, UK
www.reaktionbooks.co.uk

First published 2012, reprinted 2019

Copyright © Patricia Herlihy 2012

All rights reserved
No part of this publication may be reproduced, stored in a retrieval
system, or transmitted, in any form or by any means, electronic,
mechanical, photocopying, recording or otherwise, without the prior
permission of the publishers

Printed and bound in China by 1010 Printing International Ltd

British Library Cataloguing in Publication Data

Herlihy, Patricia
Vodka : a global history. – (Edible)
1. Vodka – History.
2. Vodka industry – History.
I. Title II. Series
641.2′5′09-DC23

ISBN 978 1 86189 929 3

Contents

Introduction:
Vodka's Intrinsic Appeal

There cannot be *too much* vodka,
there can only be *not enough* vodka.
Russian saying

Stripped to its essence, vodka is little more than pure alcohol distilled from grain – a clear liquid without colour, odour or taste. Yet, thanks to its remarkable potency and versatility, it has become the world's favourite libation. Vodka can be taken neat in one gulp *à la Russe*, or sipped as a cocktail when flavoured by almost anything palatable. Vodka can even provide the base for a refreshing drink, when combined with fruit juice, soda water, tonic or ginger beer.

One distinct advantage vodka has over its rival spirits is, to paraphrase an advertisement, that it leaves one breathless – which is a coy way of saying that it leaves no smell of liquor on one's breath. For this reason (and the fact that it looks like water), vodka is often said to have a 'clean' appeal, and is reputedly the drink of choice among tippling bartenders the world over.

Vodka also has another inherent advantage over other alcoholic drinks: affordability. Its raw materials are relatively cheap and plentiful (cultivating fields is far less labour-intensive

Moulded and enamelled glass vodka bottle. An 18th-century example of how Russians have traditionally linked romance with vodka.

than tending vineyards), and its distillation process is comparatively quick, simple and efficient. Moreover, vodka knows no vintages; there is no elaborate ageing process – after all, why would anyone bother to age a drink that is basically without taste?

Another advantage is that vodka is extremely stable and non-perishable. A Russian joke underscores this point: a drunkard enters a liquor store and asks, 'Do you have any fresh vodka today?'

The indignant merchant snaps, 'What do you mean "fresh", you idiot? It's vodka.'

'I am no idiot,' the customer retorts. 'I drank two of your bottles yesterday and they made me sick!'

Yet for all vodka's inherent simplicity, this enticing elixir defies a simple description: vodka is many things to many people. Even when taken pure, some experience no taste at all, while others detect subtle flavours imbued by the basic ingredients. Even these connoisseurs probably do not experience exactly the same sensations on their palates.

Present-day vodka makers are keenly aware of vodka's widespread appeal and marvellous marketing possibilities. They design, package and pitch their brands to target a variety of markets including women, youths, gays, macho types, *bon vivants*, connoisseurs and adventurers. Consumers, for their part, proudly proclaim their identities by their choice of brand. Vodka is, in fact, the perfect postmodern drink: marketers carefully construct a brand image while consumers define themselves – in no small part – by the brand they choose.

Most imbibers turn to vodka for pleasure, comfort, warmth, courage, consolation or even inspiration. Some maintain that it has healthful applications. As an alcoholic drink, however, it is easily abused and can be potentially a fearful, destructive force. Paradoxically, some drink vodka to heighten

Locally made vodka bottles displayed in a glass case at an airport in Kazakhstan, artfully arranged to attract the traveller's attention.

their appreciation of life's pleasures, while others use it to suppress life's pains, be they physical or emotional. Alas, it appears that one must use vodka either one way or the other, for no one can simultaneously enjoy life while seeking to escape from it.

Whatever one's take on vodka, one fact is as clear as the drink itself: this seemingly unremarkable liquid is in fact a highly potent force with both a rich history and a promising future. For centuries, poets have extolled vodka's wondrous powers, while peasants, nobles and nonentities alike have tasted its fruits and suffered its consequences. Meanwhile, a succession of authorities ranging from the Christian church

A late 19th-century advertisement for vodka. The charming young woman on the bottle hands her beau a mock prescription labelled 'Medicine for Love', calling for three doses a day to ensure a 'sparkle of love' in his eyes.

Valentine Vodka. Rifino Valentine's micro-distilled vodka made in Detroit is an example of a 21st-century boutique brand. The labels, depicting attractive women, reprise the theme that vodka enhances romance.

to the Communists have sought to control its diffusion while reaping immense revenues from popular consumption. The Russian state has always found ways to gain revenue from the production and consumption of vodka. Among the earliest producers of vodka, monks sold it for traditional purposes. Then in the 1990s President Boris Yeltsin gave the Russian Orthodox Church licence to import alcohol and sell it on the open market. Even today, vodka remains a formidable social and economic force, whether produced by artisans or by large, industrialized factories.

I

Making Vodka

Large or small, all vodka makers follow a similar process. First, they must choose their basic fermented ingredient. Traditionalists in Russia, Poland, Ukraine, Belarus, Finland, Sweden and the Baltic countries insist that only vodka made exclusively from grains, potatoes or sugar-beet molasses is worthy of the name. But distillers in Italy, France, Britain and the Netherlands take greater liberties, employing corn and various other fermentable products including fruit such as grapes and apples. They contend that vodka's base ingredients do not significantly affect its taste. In June 2007 the European Parliament passed a law that allows for a wide range of raw materials but also requires manufacturers to identify any non-traditional ingredients.

Once chosen, the basic ingredient to be fermented is crushed in a pot and mixed with water, then heated up, converting the starch into sugar. This thick wort is combined with yeast, which produces *mash*. The next step is to distil the alcoholic liquid (the *wash*) from the mash; that is, to separate the ethanol (drinking alcohol) from the other chemicals and water present in the mash. Taking advantage of the fact that alcohol comes to a boil quicker than water, distillation involves boiling the mash, then capturing the alcohol vapour through pipes into another vessel. When this vapour cools, it condenses into alcohol. However, the distiller must be careful to avoid capturing the initial vapours (the *head*), as well as the last vapours (the *tail*), which are apt to contain water or unwanted chemicals. Either these impure vapours are discarded entirely or recondensed and recombined with the distilled alcohol and then redistilled once or twice more. One distiller compares the process rather inelegantly to the refining of petrol.

Because distillation produces a highly concentrated alcoholic liquid, the vodka maker must dilute the result of the distillation process with water. How much water is added determines a very important trait of the finished vodka: its alcoholic content. The ideal alcoholic percentage of vodka constitutes yet another longstanding debate within the industry. In 1865 the great Russian scientist Dmitry Mendeleev

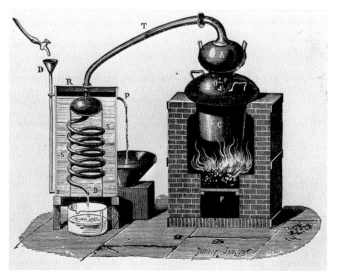

A still engraving by Dmitry Mendeleev, one of Russia's foremost scientists of the 19th century. His doctoral dissertation on vodka distillation recommended a yield close to 80 proof, a typical composition even today.

concluded in his doctoral dissertation that vodka should be 38 per cent alcohol by volume. But the figure 40 per cent became standard because it was an easier basis on which to compute taxes. More recently, the European Union has set 37.5 per cent as the minimum alcoholic content in order for the beverage to be called vodka.

Still another important variable under the distiller's control is the strength and nature of the vodka's taste, if any. Because early varieties of vodka often retained a strong and unpleasant stench (from impurities that remained in the distilled alcohol), many vodka makers have long sought to eliminate any taste whatsoever from their product. As early as the eighteenth century, Russians filtered and purified the alcohol with charcoal, an advanced method that removed excessive impurities and hence virtually all taste. Around the same time, Polish vodka distilleries supposedly introduced triple distillation, another highly effective means to purify alcohol. Even today, most mass producers, after acquiring the distilled alcohol, strive to eliminate virtually any odour, flavour or colouring. Sometimes they add coagulants to bond and reduce impurities. They may also filter the alcohol through any of a variety of substances, including sand, charcoal, lava, quartz, diamond dust, crystals and jewels, or through meshes made of stainless steel, linen, silk, French Limousin oak, cellulose or even bamboo thatches. They also use industrial-sized columns that all but eliminate the flavours coming from the mash.

Some consumers, however, prefer vodkas that retain a hint of their basic ingredient. For that reason, assert Nicholas Ermochkine and Peter Iglikowski in their recent book *40 Degrees East: An Anatomy of Vodka* (2003), Russians and Poles generally do not want their vodka distilled more than three times. To ensure some vestigial taste, many small-scale vodka makers employ pots similar to those used by moonshiners

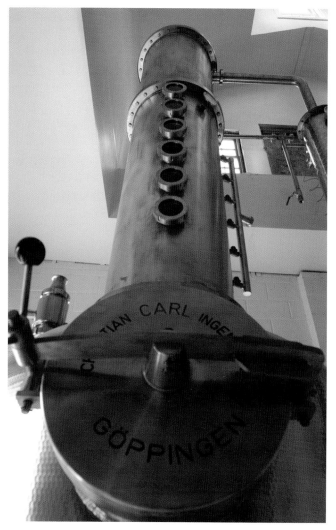

A modern copper hybrid pot and column still, a style typically used in vodka distillation before the advent of tall modern columns. Often called 'moonshine stills' because of their use during Prohibition in the USA, they are still favoured by artisanal distillers who want to retain some flavour in their product.

instead of the columns favoured by mass producers. Several American vodka makers deliberately preserve more than a hint of the original flavour of wheat or rye to give their vodka a more distinctive character.

Once the vodka maker has distilled the alcohol to the desired purity, and diluted it to the desired strength, the vodka maker must make one last decision: whether or not to *add* some kind of flavour to the drink. This ancient practice originally served to mask lingering odours, especially among smaller makers whose distilled products were generally far from tasteless. In the 1860s, for example, the famous Smirnov distillery that served the Russian royalty introduced anise and egg white additives to make their vodka more palatable to the masses. Flavourings of various sorts continue to appeal to the public, even when the unflavoured vodka itself has no taste to mask.

A contemporary bottle of Nemiroff Honey Pepper Vodka, one of Ukraine's most widely distributed brands. Russian drinkers have long favoured peppered vodka, including leaders from Peter the Great to Nikita Khrushchev.

Fayur-Soyuz vodka distillery. This modern factory in Beslan in the Republic of North Ossetia-Alania, Russia, produces 12,000 bottles per hour, even with the hand-finishing of the bottles.

Many Polish and Russian consumers, however, maintain that the best vodka is one that retains the subtle natural flavour of the base grain or potatoes, and thus has no need for added flavourings. Still others prefer to buy their vodka unflavoured, so that they can flavour the vodka as they wish.

Whether the vodka is flavoured or not, there exist no uniform international standards to measure its quality. Poland classifies vodkas according to their degree of purity: standard (*zwykła*), premium (*wyborowa*), and deluxe (*luksusowa*). Russia's labels are special (*osobaya*), which usually signifies a superior-quality product worthy of export, while strong (*krepkaya*) means vodka of at least 56 per cent alcohol. The United States government defines vodka simply as 'neutral spirits, so distilled, or so treated after distillation with charcoal or other materials, as to be without distinctive character, aroma, taste or color'. Ultra- and super-premium brands are generally subjected to more frequent distillation and filtration, resulting in a smoother vodka that can be drunk neat. They are generally marketed in elaborate bottles and cost between 50 per cent and 100 per cent more than premium brands.

Many vodka companies claim a superior product simply by virtue of the water used to dilute the alcohol after distillation. Often distilled or deionised water is used for this purpose, but ideally the water comes from pure lakes or glacial springs. And while vodka itself is not usually aged, some makers boast that their water is. The potato-based Alaskan vodka Permafrost draws its water from a 10,000-year-old glacier in Prince William Sound. Canada's Iceberg Vodka counters that its source, 12,000-year-old icebergs, yields the purest waters. As if to top that claim, 26000 Vodka states that its 'lovingly crafted' and hand-bottled product is distilled with water from an underground spring in New Zealand that is over 26,000 years old.

In short, the smoothness and taste of vodka, or lack thereof, depends on its basic ingredients, the distillation process, in particular the frequency and type of filtration and the purity

Permafrost Vodka, made in Alaska. Advertisements stress that their distillation process employs only the purest water from glacial ice, thereby ensuring top quality.

of the water added to dilute the ethanol, as well as the choice of added flavouring, if any. But what constitutes the ideal ingredients, process and final product is strictly a matter of personal taste.

2
Not Just for Drinking

Given the present popularity of vodka as a social drink, it is easy to overlook the fact that, historically at least, it has been much more than a recreational beverage. Developed centuries ago by monks as an elixir, vodka has long been imbibed for medicinal purposes, especially in Russia.

In *Mirgorod*, an 1835 collection of short stories, Nikolai Gogol described one peasant's unshakeable faith in vodka's curative powers:

> Pulkheria Ivanovna was most entertaining when she led her guests to the zakuska [hors d'oeuvres] table. 'Now this,' she would say, removing the stopper from a flask, 'is vodka infused with St John's wort and sage. If the small of your back or your shoulder blade aches, it really hits the spot. This vodka over here is made with centaury. If you've got a ringing in your ears or shingles on your face, it's just the thing. And this one's distilled from peach pits here, take a glass, what a wonderful smell! If you've bumped your head against the corner of a cupboard or the table when getting out of bed, and a lump's sprung up on your forehead, then all you have to do is drink a glassful before dinner. The minute you take your hand

away, the lump will disappear, as if it had never been there
at all.'

In the Soviet era, vodka was often proffered as a cure-all. A
tall glass with two teaspoons of black pepper was widely
believed to cure colds. Even today, a Canadian firm, Signature, produces a clear spirit using an infusion process with
curcumin enzymes. Curcuma, which includes the turmeric
species, is widely renowned for its many medical benefits.

Most traditional health-related applications of vodka,
however, do not actually require imbibing the liquid. A friend
of mine recalls an amusing incident from 1981, when he was
a graduate student living in Boston suffering from a painful
ear infection. A family of Soviet émigrés appeared at his bed-
side to implement a cure. He relates:

> Their Soviet folk remedy went like this: boil vodka. Soak
> a thick piece of cotton gauze in it. Cover the gauze with
> wax paper. Press the ensemble against the sore ear by
> means of a thick wool scarf wrapped around the head
> and tied under the chin. To ensure that the vodka fumes
> penetrated the ear, the procedure was supposed to be
> repeated every few hours. Had it not been so oppressively

Signature Vodka, made in Canada with pure spring water and infused with
antioxidants to ward off hangovers.

hot that day, I might have humoured them, just to see what happened. But the scarf was so itchy and uncomfortable that I could not bear it for long. About an hour after the Russians left, I stripped it off and bolted from my bed. Thanks to my doctor-prescribed antibiotics, I was soon pain-free. But when the Russians called on me the next day to see how I was doing, I dared not reveal the truth. Instead, I assured them that the vodka-soaked headdress had indeed worked its magic. Otherwise I would never have heard the end of it.

Soviets also used vodka as a prophylactic before testing any radioactive material, as it was widely believed to stop the absorption of radioisotopes. In Ukraine many drank vodka in the aftermath of the Chernobyl nuclear power plant explosion of 1986, hoping to cleanse their systems of the harmful effects. At least one brand, Doktor Vodka, suggests on its label that it has curative powers.

Even today, Russians and other East Europeans use vodka in a variety of home remedies. Some apply it to cold sores to dry them up, while others gargle a concoction of vodka and hot water to soothe a sore throat or ease the pain of a toothache, supposedly disinfecting the trouble spot in the process.

Russians, however, are by no means the only ones who employ vodka for healthful purposes. To guard against the spread of the flu virus, the Very Reverend Steve Lipscomb, dean of Grace Episcopal Cathedral in Topeka, Kansas, wipes down his chalices after every use with vodka-soaked gauze. He explains, 'Obviously, if you are wiping with 80-proof alcohol, you are probably being about as safe as you can be.' Campers who happen to have a supply of vodka on hand often use it to sterilize instruments or to disinfect wounds inflicted by

Doktor Vodka.
A Slovak product,
the red cross
suggests a med-
icinal property.
Chernobyl residents
reportedly drank
this brand in the
aftermath of the
nuclear disaster to
offset any radiation
effects.

hostile creatures ranging from dogs to jellyfish. Some adventurers have even been known to use vodka to repel bugs or to
soothe itches stemming from poison ivy and the like.

Some claim that a washcloth soaked in vodka and applied
to the chest can help relieve the effects of a fever. For a good
old-fashioned liniment, herbalists suggest that you put some
sprigs of lavender in a jar, fill it with vodka, and then set it
out in the sun for several days. The resulting balm is said to
soothe general aches and pains. One can also create an ice-
pack by freezing a plastic zipped bag filled with equal parts of
water and vodka.

Vodka can also be used for personal hygiene. Some
women apply vodka as an astringent to the face, to remove oil

and tighten pores. Several over-the-counter facial and body scrub lotions use vodka as a base. Vodka mixed with powdered cinnamon then strained can provide a refreshing mouthwash. To create your own perfume, you can fill your vial with an ounce of vodka mixed with 20 to 30 drops of an oil essence, taking care to let the mixture sit for several weeks before use. To eliminate foot odours, you can soak your feet in diluted vodka. Immersing a razor blade in a vodka solution after use is said to prevent rust. Eyeglasses and jewellery can be cleaned with vodka solutions. Vodka added to your favourite shampoo will eliminate the build-up of soapy residue on hair. To eliminate dandruff, some recommend soaking rosemary in a vodka solution and letting the mixture sit for a few days before filtering it and applying it to the scalp.

Housekeepers also make good use of vodka, diluting it with water and using the solution as a spray to polish glass and chrome surfaces, including mirrors, ceramic tiles and even chandeliers. In 2011 some 150 gilders applied a medieval recipe of Russian vodka, gold leaf and egg whites to restore the gilt in Moscow's famous Bolshoi Theatre.

More commonly, however, vodka solutions are used as cleansing agents. They can remove mould and mildew on bathroom caulking, and mud and grass stains on carpets, if the solution is left to dry and then vacuumed up. It is said that vodka can even clean carbon off spark plugs. Vodka solutions can also eliminate stains and odours on clothing, when sprayed on affected areas. The wardrobe mistress at the San Francisco Opera House freshens costumes after every use in this manner.

A complete list of possible uses of vodka solutions would be extensive. Adding vodka and sugar to water at the base of Christmas trees or to vases of flowers is thought to prolong the life of the plants. Vebjørn Sand, a Norwegian artist, has devised an especially creative and specialized use for it. Visiting Antarctica, he attempted to paint outdoor scenes, but his watercolours kept freezing. Finally, at the urging of Russian guides, he solved the problem by adding a touch of vodka. He now calls his process vodka colour.

In 2009 an American blogger speculated on what he should do if there was a collapse of the paper dollar. He noted that one of his friends had already prepared for such an emergency by stocking up on small bottles of vodka to use as a medium of exchange. However ingenious his friend's idea might be, it was hardly innovative. Bartering with vodka has long been a common practice within the former Soviet Union, from tsarist to recent times, in much the way that Native Americans had traditionally used beads as wampum.

In tsarist Russia employers were so accustomed to paying their workers with bottles of vodka that the government outlawed the practice. Still, distillers continued to hand out bottles to their workers, including children, as partial payment or to

The main stage of the magnificent Bolshoi Theatre, a cultural landmark closed in 2005 for renovation after years of neglect. To regild the ornate interior, restorers are employing a medieval recipe involving eggs, gold leaf and vodka.

reward productivity. For their part, workers occasionally gifted their bosses bottles of vodka in hopes of improving their working conditions.

When vodka was scarce, as it was in August 1914 following Nicolas II's ban on vodka to ensure that recruits for the First World War would turn up sober, or in times of economic turmoil, such as the hyperinflation that afflicted Russia after the war, vodka, along with moonshine and bread, has often been preferred over currency as a medium of exchange. After all, vodka is portable, durable and, above all, desirable. During the Second World War, especially in Leningrad, which was undergoing a famine while under siege, bread and vodka became once again the major currencies.

In the Soviet period vodka became relatively cheap and plentiful. For ordinary Russians the usual brands of vodka available in the 1960s were a half-litre bottle of Moskovskaya

Moskovskaya Russian Vodka, a brand that dates back to 1894, when the State Vodka Monopoly was created.

for 2.87 rubles or a slightly better bottle of Stolichnaya for 3.12 rubles. Also obtainable but in less supply were Zubrówka (bison grass), Polynnaya (absinthe) and Starka, one of the rare vodkas that is aged in oak barrels for about ten years.

Still, given the scarcity of consumer goods, Soviet service workers often preferred to be paid with good vodka rather than rubles. In fact the phrase for a tip, *na chai*, means 'for tea' but more often in Russia, at any period, tea money meant vodka money. According to the Moscow Vodka Museum, in Siberia at one time even vodka labels were used as cash, but surely for a limited time.

More recently, Chechen rebels have offered vodka bottles to Russian soldiers in exchange for bullets and guns. Some of the supplies were allegedly tainted with bleach, so as to blind the enemy recipients. It is said that Russian gravediggers are still paid in bottles of vodka, enabling them to toast the departed.

Robert Parsons, writing for Radio Free Europe/Radio Liberty in August 2006, reported that Tatarstan suffered a severe shortage of vodka, after passing a law requiring vendors to obtain licences. The measure effectively drove the small shops and kiosks out of business. Suddenly, vodka became a valuable currency, especially in small villages. No services, large or small, would be rendered without payment in vodka as long as the drought lasted.

Increasingly, even empty vodka bottles are being put to good use the world over. A few private citizens have reportedly made small fortunes by recycling vodka bottles. In October 2009 Leonid Konovalov told a Russian newspaper that he successfully exploited the recent surge in drinking sparked by the downturn of the economy by collecting an average of 2,000 empty vodka bottles a day (at 6 US cents a bottle). He had amassed so much wealth that he was allegedly ready to leave

Many aficionados of vodka collect bottles. This Polish connoisseur specializes in miniature varieties.

the rubbish business and head for the stock market (cynics, especially Communists, might see a certain continuity there). In the interest of a cleaner environment and reduced expenses, the Great Lakes Distillery of Milwaukee, Wisconsin, is urging customers to return their empty bottles for cleaning and reuse.

Certain bottles have become quite collectible as *objets d'art*, due to their distinctive shapes or material composition. In addition, bits and pieces of vodka bottles have been incorporated into art projects, some of which are displayed in museums. California's Transportation Department crushes Skyy Vodka's cobalt-blue bottles and distributes the colourful remains along Interstate 5 near Sacramento to beautify the landscape.

Even photographs of artistic bottles constitute a form of art, as for example in striking and at times humorous vodka advertisements. The first Absolut ad, *Absolut Perfection*, appeared in 1980. Since then more than 1,500 notable advertisements have followed. Andy Warhol was the first artist to collaborate with Absolut in 1985 and Spike Jonze, the American film director, is one of the more recent.

The latest stars to lend their scantily clad figures to the famous series of Absolut ads are Kate Beckinsale and Zooey Deschanel, photographed by Ellen von Unwerth. In commemoration of all the artists who helped make the brand famous, the vodka company awards an annual Art Award (€15,000 and a chance to collaborate in company projects) to an international young artist exploring creativity through the integration of art forms. About 800 pieces of artwork produced for the company will be housed in Stockholm at the Historical Museum of Wine and Spirits.

For Level Vodka, a super-premium brand made by the same producers of Absolut, fashion designer and artist Hussein Chalayan created a tunnel fifteen metres (49 feet) long and five metres (16 feet) high with a soft leather railing, through which visitors wander blindfolded, listening to musical flutes made of Level bottles, sniffing the scent of the vodka and finally tasting the beverage after emerging from the immersion experience.

3
Vodka the Terrible

For all its appeal as a libation and as a cure-all, vodka is nevertheless a highly dangerous and potentially destructive force. There is simply no denying that alcohol abuse has become a pressing global issue in which vodka plays no small role. A recent University of Toronto study determined that one in 25 deaths across the world is linked to excessive alcohol consumption. In Russia excessive consumption of vodka has been associated with the 'demographic crisis', that is, the high mortality rate, especially for men of working age and low fertility.

Much of the problem, no doubt, is the extraordinary degree to which Russians have become inured to the dangers of vodka. Vitalii Krichevskii of St Petersburg, author of *Russian Vodka*, has verified 3,828 distinct words and expressions that invoke the potent libation, many of which reveal a high level of acceptance of its abuse. One common adage is: 'Vodka is the enemy of the people, but the people are not afraid of the enemy', or 'Vodka is the enemy of the people and we shall consume the enemy'.

But, of course, the legacy of vodka abuse is no laughing matter. While some Poles of yore hailed the drink as an aphrodisiac that contributed to population growth, vodka's actual effect can be to lower life expectancy.

To be sure, vodka is not the only alcoholic substance commonly abused. Many young people in Russia tote large bottles of beer at all times of the day or night, as if they were bottles of water. According to some experts, young people are consuming ever larger quantities of beer and other low-alcohol drinks. At present, about one-third of Russian young men drink beer daily or every other day, as do one-fifth of young Russian women.

On average, every year a Russian citizen buys 81 litres of beer, 14.3 litres of vodka, cognac and other strong alcohol, and 6 litres of wine – a total of 101.3 litres of licensed alcohol, or 18 litres of pure alcohol. 'This is equivalent to about 50 bottles of vodka for each resident of the country, including infants', Russia's President Dmitry Medvedev has observed. 'This is a

In the mid-16th century Ivan IV (the Terrible) sought to enhance his power by limiting access to vodka to all but his most ardent supporters. This boutique Russian brand uses an exotic recipe from that period, infusing wild buckwheat honey and Siberian cedar nuts.

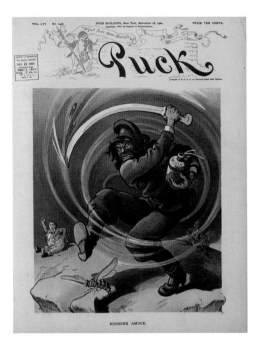

Cover of *Puck* magazine evoking the ongoing Russo–Japanese War, 1904. As an alarmed John Bull and Uncle Sam look on, a drunken giant clutching a jug of vodka (Russia) attempts to slay a wasp (Japan). The suggestion is that the Russian decision to wage war against Japan may have been ill-advised.

monstrous figure. After 9–10 litres, gene pool problems arise, and degradation begins.'

Proclaiming the situation 'a national disaster' in 2011, Medvedev has called for a variety of measures designed to reduce alcohol consumption in Russia, especially among young people. These would include raising the drinking age to 21 years, enforcing strict criminal penalties for those who sell alcohol to minors and restricting the sale of alcohol in supermarkets, cafes and restaurants located within a certain distance from schools, healthcare facilities and sports centres. If enacted, thousands of small street kiosks, which currently sell fortified beer and other hard liquors, would be banned.

Other commonly proposed measures would be to enforce stricter quality standards as well as to raise taxes, especially on vodka. At present, nearly half of the vodka consumed in Russia is illegally produced, and thus of dubious quality. The idea of raising the minimum price of a half-litre bottle of vodka to 89 rubles (about $3), however, does not sit well with the Russian public.

Somewhat more politically palatable, given that about two-thirds of the beer consumed in Russia is foreign-made, is a recent proposal to increase the tax on beer by 11 per cent in 2011, and 20 per cent in 2012. Some have expressed concern, however, that if beer were to become almost as expensive as vodka, consumption of the latter would rise even higher and the effects of alcohol abuse would worsen.

Some suggest that the solution to the problem is for drinkers to confine their intake of hard liquor to premium vodka. Proponents of this approach argue that, first, the better the vodka, the less likely that it will be consumed to excess

Russian moonshine paraphernalia, early 20th century. Russian citizens, to the present day, have long employed simple devices to produce illegal vodka, especially during the prohibition of 1914–25.

and, second, that the effects of over-consuming quality vodka are in any case more benign than those imposed by comparable hard liquors. This notion seems to be taking hold in Russia. Some upscale restaurants feature as many as 40 different premium brands. The premise of the Vodka Museum in Uglich near the Volga river is also to educate Russians so that they become connoisseurs of fine vodka rather than compulsive drinkers who are indifferent to its quality.

One possible response to the current alcohol crisis would be the re-establishment of the State Vodka Monopoly that Boris Yeltsin abolished in 1992. This prospect is especially tempting to bureaucrats, given the declining revenues generated by the export of gas and oil. Their pretext, no doubt, would be the same as in 1894: to ensure the quality of vodka and to curb excessive consumption. But the result might lead, once again, to increased alcoholism because the price would be low

Soviet Temperance poster. Rampant alcoholism was a chronic problem throughout the Soviet era. To promote sobriety, the state commissioned skilled graphic artists to produce anti-alcohol posters. This one depicts an inverse relationship between alcohol consumption and productivity. The caption reads, 'A friend of vodka is the enemy of the professional unions.'

and the quality high, encouraging people to purchase more vodka. The state might also encourage more sales to increase revenue. And if the present leaders try to crack down too hard on moonshiners, as did Nicholas II in 1914 and Mikhail Gorbachev in 1985, or worse yet, attempt to effect any kind of ban on alcohol, they might quickly find themselves out of power.

And so it is that vodka continues its Jekyll and Hyde performance, providing the world with a wonderful – if not miraculous – substance, while at the same time exacting a terrible toll on those who abuse it.

4
Origins

Centuries ago vodka originated somewhere in Eastern Europe, in the region now comprising Russia, Poland, Belarus and Ukraine. Unable to grow grapes in their frigid climate, the locals sought to create a new libation from cheap and plentiful wheat, one that could match the intoxicating qualities of *aqua vitae* and wine. The first distillers were probably Russian and Polish monks, who dispensed their pungent concoctions primarily as medicine (sedative, anaesthesia, liniment and disinfectant).

By the fifteenth century distillers had introduced new variations distilled from other grains such as rye, oats, barley and buckwheat. And, as they improved their art, they managed to reduce the nasty smell of their vodka and mask any lingering unpleasantness by infusing their output with honey, fruit, spices, herbs and berries. Although these developments did not necessarily enhance vodka's reputed medicinal qualities, they did ensure that it became an increasingly palatable and popular drink.

By the sixteenth century many more flavourings had been introduced, including pepper, gypsy rose, valerian root, sandalwood, gold leaf and anise. Poland alone offered at least 72 herbal vodkas, in addition to one made with the juice of a marinated adder, called *Zmijowka*. Meanwhile, vodka consumption spread across northern Europe, the Baltic and Scandinavian countries, Finland, Iceland and Greenland.

For several centuries vodka remained largely confined to northern climes. But its magic could not remain bottled up in that region indefinitely. In the nineteenth and twentieth centuries vodka steadily spilled southward, before spreading further to the east and west. Today, it can be found virtually anywhere on the globe.

The emergence of vodka on the world stage and the resurgence of nationalism in Russia and Poland has rekindled a long-running debate as to which of those two countries originated this powerful, pleasurable and at times poisonous potable. The Russians proudly declare it to be their offspring – pointing out that the word itself comes from the Russian word *voda*, meaning water. The Poles counter that *wodka*, derived from *woda*, their word for water, is actually their love child. Scott Simpson has argued that the Polish word *wodka*

Ukrainian Vodka Khlibnii Dar, meaning Wheat's Gift Vodka. A fancy display at the airport in Kyiv entices travellers to buy duty-free bottles.

for the product, as we know it, appeared before the Russian word *vodka* was used for that same alcoholic drink. A contemporary advertisement for the Polish Sobieski vodka declares:

> An announcement for those prepared to have their
> illusions shattered:
> Vodka originated in Poland.
> Sorry about that, Russia.

In fact, some Polish historians maintain that the first identifiable vodka appeared in their country as early as the eleventh century. It was called *gorzalka*, a word deriving from the Polish verb 'to burn', meaning that, if lit by a flame, the alcohol burned. Russian historians, however, insist that this was not true vodka, but rather a more primitive distilled drink like *aqua vitae*.

In truth, it is difficult to discern a bona fide vodka production in either country much before the fifteenth century. This is affirmed by the late Russian historian William Pokhlebkin, who traced the origins of vodka to the Moscow region: 'The advent of grain spirit, a genuinely new product, could not have occurred earlier than the second half of the fourteenth century.'

Still, there is no doubt that Poles were indeed imbibing their own varieties by the fifteenth century. But since there is also irrefutable evidence of Russian vodka production in the same period, the matter of priority remains highly opaque. Nor can one rule out the distinct possibility that a third party introduced vodka to the general region. According to one such theory, western mercenaries fighting for Russia imported vodka for their own discreet consumption. The Russians, however, discovered their secret indulgence and learned how to make the libation themselves.

Be that as it may, it is highly likely that foreigners taught both the Russians and Poles the art of distillation. Among the possible mentors were Germanic Hanseatic traders, who in 1259 established a trading post in Novgorod in northwestern Russia, and Genoese colonists who settled in the Crimea in the fourteenth century and introduced *aqua vitae*. Some

Sobieski Vodka. A Polish advertisement taunting Russia about the true origin of vodka, an age-old debate that might never be resolved.

Fireweed Vodka, made by Alaska Distillery. An example of one of the many flavoured artisan vodkas, popular with contemporary consumers who desire colourful cocktails.

have also suggested that Tatars may have taught Russians how to distil a fermented product.

For their part, Ukrainians also claim to be the originators of vodka. They point to archaeological evidence showing that distillation took place on their land as early as the fifteenth century. They also observe that as the largest regional producer of grains at the time it would hardly be surprising if they had been the first to produce vodka. Known then and now as *horilka*, similar to the Polish word *gorzalka* and the Belarusian *harelka*, it also derived from the verb 'to burn'.

Perhaps all that we can safely distil from the origins controversy is that the West probably introduced a distilled concoction to the East that served as the inspiration for vodka. The East, in turn, developed vodka and exported it back to the West.

Whether or not it originated vodka, Poland has long played a crucial role in its development and diffusion. In 1534 a Polish herbalist extolled the virtues of *wodka*, noting that it aroused lust and thus increased fertility. By the early sixteenth century Polish distillers had begun to export their product. The towns of Posnan and Krakow emerged as the centres of domestic vodka production, before Gdansk eventually overtook them. By 1620 numerous Polish cities were dispensing distilling privileges. In that year alone officials in Gdansk sold 68 licences to individuals.

Polish distillers also developed new production techniques and flavours. In 1693 the distiller Jakub Kazimierz Haur, based in Krakow, published recipes describing how to make vodka out of rye rather than the traditional wheat. In the early nineteenth century Poland introduced the plentiful potato as an alternative base ingredient. By 1836, in Galicia alone, the Austrian sector of partitioned Poland, some 4,981 distilleries were flourishing. By 1844 another 2,094 distilleries were operating in the Russian sector, known as the Kingdom of Poland. Polish nobles also took to distilling vodka on their estates.

Of course the Polish industry did not always enjoy growth and prosperity. Between 1843 and 1851 the European potato blight severely curtailed production. And in the 1870s the Russians imposed a hefty excise tax on Polish-produced vodka sold within the Russian Empire, stifling production and destroying all but the largest and most efficient Polish distilleries.

Since then, however, the Polish vodka industry has flourished, becoming a world leader in production and innovation. One of its highly coveted creations is Bak's Bison Grass Vodka, an offshoot of an older concoction called Zubrówka. Since bison, like bulls, are symbols of virility, some claim that this yellowish drink enhances virility (ironically Polish men

Bison Grass Vodka label. A favourite of Poles and Russians, this bison grass-infused vodka is reputed to enhance men's virility. In fact, the grass can act as an anti-coagulant, which forced exporters to modify the formula.

Zubrówka Vodka. A favourite Polish brand of bison grass, yellowish vodka served with ice. It is said to appeal to women.

allegedly dismiss it as a woman's drink). For decades, US officials, perhaps fearing that it really was an aphrodisiac, blocked its importation – or perhaps it was because bison grass also produces coumarin, an anticoagulant, making the drink potentially harmful. The ban was finally lifted in 2009, and it remains to be seen whether the drink will produce a spurt in the American birth rate.

The Russian vodka industry has likewise experienced tremendous growth and diversification over the years. By the nineteenth century Russian housewives were routinely making their own vodka, and many households today still offer their own homemade varieties. Although the trend in Russia, as elsewhere, is toward ever larger and more mechanized distilleries, high quality artisanal offerings remain a source of national pride. Even the small-scale tax-evading moonshiner has not disappeared entirely.

5
Vodka and the Tsars

Ever since vodka was established in Russia, and the industry began to grow, Russian regimes have repeatedly sought to control production and to tax consumption. In 1474 Ivan III (1440–1505) established the first state vodka monopoly. Called 'Great' because of his successful expansion of Muscovite rule, he relied heavily on vodka-generated tax revenues to wage his wars of conquest (though he mistakenly believed that he could contain alcoholism simply by limiting the amount of vodka produced).

His successor, Ivan IV (The Terrible, 1530–1583), likewise understood that he could enhance his power by controlling the robust vodka industry. In his struggle against nobles whom he deemed a threat to his authority, Ivan created a new privileged class called the *oprichniki* to replace the old aristocracy. In order to ensure their loyalty, he not only gave them land, but also exclusive access to the prized liquid. In 1544 he established eight taverns (*kabaki*) selling strong spirits only to his newly created servitors. But if they failed to obey his orders, they were cut off.

No Russian ruler better understood the power of vodka than Peter the Great (1672–1725). He used the liquid to reward his loyal supporters, to subdue his adversaries and to punish his enemies. He frequently plied his foreign guests with vodka to loosen their lips. Some, however, were so unaccustomed to such a potent libation that they soon slumped senseless on the table or simply dropped dead. He would also force his enemies to drink vodka to excess. He even used the liquid to test aspiring ambassadors. Only those who could still speak sensibly after imbibing a bucket of vodka were admitted into the Tsar's foreign service.

In 1695 Peter created the Drunken Council of Fools and Jesters, in part to quench his own insatiable thirst for vodka. According to the first commandment he himself decreed, the band was 'to get drunk every day and never go to bed sober'. Not only did Peter enjoy watching their vodka-induced buffoonery, he also became a willing participant in their parties, parades and parodies. In one particularly irreverent skit, he dressed as a lowly deacon, while the chief buffoon played the part of the Prince-Pope and a dozen drunks represented the College of Cardinals. Vodka was used as holy water and the ensemble belted out bawdy parodies of sacred hymns. Peter's death at the relatively young age of 53 was no doubt hastened by his own prodigious consumption of the drink.

In the late eighteenth century, thanks to the abstemious Catherine II (The Great, 1729–1796), the common people, including serfs, gradually gained access to vodka. She abolished the state monopoly and authorized the government to auction a limited number of licences to produce and sell vodka at a low, fixed price. But although availability increased as a result, the general quality of the drink was often compromised. The so-called tax farmers who produced vodka, in order to recoup the large sums that they had paid upfront, diluted and sold as much of their adulterated vodka as the market would bear.

The common folk had relatively limited opportunities to imbibe, given the heavy burden of farming. Because of

Russia's harsh northern climate, the growing season is short. Serfs, before their emancipation in 1861, and peasants thereafter, were constantly racing against time to till the earth, sow seeds and reap their crops. As an American traveller in the summer of 1880 noted, their days were long and arduous: 'Peasants were seen in long lines coming from the fields in the twilight at half-past eight and nine o'clock, and they had begun work at four in the morning.' Rarely did they have the time or resources to indulge in drinking during the most intensive spurts of agricultural activity.

Even after they had stored their crops and collected their pay, they were expected to confine their drinking to appropriate celebratory occasions, like holy days, which generally fell, not coincidentally, in the late autumn, winter and early spring, when the demands of farming were relatively light.

Natalia Goncharova, *Peasant with Flask*. A Russian avant-garde artist, Goncharova emigrated after the 1917 Revolution to France, where she designed costumes for Sergei Diaghilev's Ballets Russes. This one was designed for *Le Coq D'Or*, staged in Paris in 1914.

Despite these constraints, peasants managed to consume large quantities of vodka in the course of a typical year. In fact, binge drinking was already a well-known social plague by tsarist times. Though fictional, Anton Chekhov's village of Zhukovo would hardly have been an anomaly. The author bluntly described the villagers' drinking habits:

> On Elijah's Day they drank. On the feast of the Assumption they drank. On Holy Cross Day they drank. The feast of the Intercession was the parish holiday for Zhukovo and the villagers seized the chance to drink for three days.

Significant milestones of life, such as births, baptisms, weddings, funerals or the induction of a son into the army, afforded additional pretexts for boozy celebrations, and were especially welcome when they fell during the long, dark winters. The sealing of business deals and the occasional visit from friends and family also required offerings of vodka.

An American Presbyterian minister, while visiting Russia around 1880, observed:

> Drunkenness is the great vice of the people. I saw more drunken men in Russia than I have seen in any part of continental Europe. Not a day passed without painful exhibitions of men in almost every station of life, who were intoxicated or helplessly drunk. The people love strong liquors, and the lower classes drink a villainous fiery liquor called 'vodki' [sic], which is worse than a torchlight procession going down the throat.

Wealthy nobles and the landowning gentry were likewise expected to confine their drinking to holy days, important family events and the entertaining of honoured guests. But

Cut glass decanters and a Bros Crachev imperial crystal vodka bottle with silver mounts. Made for the Grand Duke Pavel Aleksandrovich of Russia, the bottle comes with its own silver shot glass, and was made in St Petersburg around 1900.

since they were far more accustomed to receiving visitors, they had even more opportunities to imbibe, perhaps justifying the popular saying, 'the rich drink when they will, but the poor only when they can'.

Naturally, the rich also enjoyed the very best vodka. Aristocrats were keenly aware that the quantity and quality of their vodka reflected on their status. Nearly every prominent household proudly offered its guests its own variety of vodka, homemade according to the favourite family recipe. One contemporary Russian chef described the assortment of flavourings commonly served in wealthier households: 'white orange, red orange, bitter orange, mint, almond, peach, clove, raspberry, cherry, balsamic, rose, anise, wormwood, gold, cinnamon, lemon and caraway vodka'.

Then, as now, the only social requirement is that one must never drink without also ingesting food. Typically, the hosts poured vodka from elaborate decanters made of tinted glass or, occasionally, from chilled bottles, into decorated tumblers or *charki* made of precious metals (peasants, in contrast, typically drank from simpler *stopki* made of cheaper materials). The guests, meanwhile, helped themselves to an assortment of hors d'oeuvres called *zakuski*: caviar, pickled herrings, smoked ham, tongue and a wide variety of smoked fish, bread, butter, cheese, mushrooms and tiny pastries filled with fish, cabbage or meat as well as perhaps a dish of chopped mushrooms, nuts and onions. A lavish meal followed and the ensemble would continue to down gulps of vodka with each new, elaborate toast, a ritual that survives to this day. Wine and cognacs were also offered.

Anton Chekhov described how refined Russians were expected to drink vodka:

> When you sit down you should immediately put a napkin around your neck and then, very slowly, reach for the carafe of vodka. Now you don't pour the dear stuff into any old glass . . . oh no! You must pour it into an

Antip Kuzmichev, six silver-gilt and cloisonné vodka cups. Known as charkas, these special cups were used by the rich to serve vodka to their dinner or party guests. The poor used simpler and less expensive variations.

antediluvian glass made of silver, one that belonged to your grandfather, or into a pot-bellied glass bearing the inscription 'Even Monks Imbibe!' And you don't drink the vodka down right away. No, sir. First you take a deep breath, wipe your hands, and glance up at the ceiling to demonstrate your indifference. Only then do you raise that vodka slowly to your lips and suddenly, sparks! They fly from your stomach to the furthest reaches of your body.

Over the years, vodka has contributed not only to Russian social customs but also to both its material and fine arts. Given the importance ascribed to imbibing rituals, the manufacturing of vodka containers, bottles and cups has long been an art form. In the nineteenth and early twentieth century numerous manufacturers, including the famous Fabergé Company,

Fabergé enamel tumbler, vodka cups and a bowl, early 20th century. Famous for its bejewelled eggs destined for tsars and aristocrats, Fabergé also made elaborate vodka paraphernalia, proving that vodka consumption was not confined to peasants and workers.

produced highly elaborate vodka bottles, carafes and glasses. Thanks to Russia's vast natural resources, including mines in the Ural and Caucasus mountains and in Siberia, they had their pick of precious materials to work with, including silver, gold, nephrite, rhodonite and agate.

Russian and resident foreign artisans fashioned lovely carafes, flasks and vodka cups or *charkas*. Vodka cups were made of silver gilt niello or green, blue or salmon-pink enamel. Others were made from cloisonné enamel, as well as of agate, silver, rhodonite, red or yellow gold and clear or tinted glass. Some cups were highly ornamented, as beloved objects often are. Exquisite cups of fine gold or silver sometimes sported handles made of bear claws in the shape of a toucan. Others had finely wrought handles in the shape of a snake with ruby eyes. The serpent, symbolizing alcohol, was a frequent motif. Enamelled *charkas* sometimes were of solid colours or of decorative patterns comprised of flowers, goldfish or birds.

Vodka also influenced painting. In the nineteenth century a school of artists called the Itinerants or the Wanderers (*Peredvizhniki*) turned away from classical themes to depict the realities of Russian life. Among the subjects was the use and misuse of vodka. Vasily Perov (1834–1882) in his painting *A Meal in the Monastery* depicted well-nourished monks enjoying abundant food along with copious vodka, while groaning beggars plead for alms around the table. *The Last Tavern at Town Gate* depicts a pub buried in snow. Outside sits a peasant woman in a cart, presumably waiting for her male companion to finish his last drink 'for the road'. Perov's *Easter Procession in a Village* offers a scathing denunciation of clerical drunkenness: a priest staggers off a porch as he attempts to join inebriated peasants in a religious procession, holding his icon upside down.

Vasiliy Perov, *A Meal in the Monastery*, 1865–76. A member of a school of painting known as The Wanderers, Perov depicted realistic and often critical scenes of daily life in Russia. Here he shows well-fed monks feasting and drinking while a man and a woman with ragged children are begging for alms.

Another artist of the same genre, Leonid Ivanovich Solomatkin (1837–1883), painted realistic drinking scenes with titles such as *The Pub, Morning at the Tavern: The Golden Bank* and *Merchant Evening Party*. The latter shows a table filled with *zakuski* and bottles of vodka. A servant girl is passing around an open bottle of vodka and shot glasses to the guests who are enjoying a musical evening, although one of the partygoers has already passed out.

The famous Soviet poet and artist Vladimir V. Maiakovskii shows in one of his paintings a woman with a small boy clinging to her, her arms outstretched against a tavern door, crying out to her ragged husband on the approach, 'I shall not let you in here.' He also drew a vicious critique of the State Vodka Monopoly under the tsarist regime. Nicholas and Alexandra are shown sitting on a throne, with a carved vodka bottle replacing the traditional double-headed eagle.

The royal couple holds bottles of vodka. At their feet are pots overflowing with coins and drunkards lying about. In the background are vodka factories belching out smoke. The less than subtle message: the state was as addicted to vodka revenues as the people were to vodka itself.

Russian poster art also conveyed strong, anti-alcohol messages. The artists, however, generally shunned realism, employing instead the fine tradition of graphic art. In tsarist times they often infused their anti-vodka imagery with anti-religious propaganda. The tradition continued into the Soviet era. One famous poster depicts Jesus as a moonshiner.

For its part, Russian literature is saturated with vodka references. Feodor Dostoevsky, for one, alludes to excessive drinking and its toll in nearly all of his novels. In *Crime and Punishment* (1866), originally entitled *The Drunkards*, he depicts the filthy, dark taverns of St Petersburg. The heroine Sonia, whose father is a hopeless alcoholic, is forced into prostitution in order to support her younger siblings. Similarly, the novels and short stories of Ivan Turgenev and Chekhov reveal how deeply vodka drinking is woven into the texture of Russian life. Maxim Gorky with a more critical eye also depicts in his plays and novels the depths of Russian drunkenness.

By the early 1890s many Russians had become addicted to vodka; some were even dying from impure varieties. Growing numbers of priests, officers, doctors, teachers, socialists, women and other lay groups prodded the tsarist regime to take vigorous steps to curtail vodka consumption and thereby suppress rampant public drunkenness. Even Alexander III (1845–1894), who was notoriously scornful of public opinion, could not ignore their increasingly vocal demands. Moreover, chronic alcoholism threatened his massive industrialization programme, which required a large pool of sober workers. He thus reversed the liberal policy initiated by Catherine II more than a century earlier and reinstated the state monopoly to limit production and impose rigid quality standards.

The Tsar, himself a heavy drinker, oversaw the creation of an official Temperance Society, called The Guardianship of Public Sobriety, to be funded by the state monopoly and staffed by government officials. Unlike the typical privately organized Temperance societies, which were often headed by zealots who demanded a total ban on vodka, the state agency advocated moderate consumption, or what we might today call 'responsible drinking'. Reasoning that it could curb abuse of alcohol by elevating popular culture, the agency hired playwrights and provided the masses with free entertainment in public theatres. Workers were also treated to concerts, outings, literacy classes and even cheap food and lodgings to facilitate leisure travel.

Despite these measures, the problem of widespread alcohol abuse not only persisted, but actually worsened. Although the state stores generally served a better grade of vodka than the taverns they supplanted, in contrast to the latter, they did not serve food. Patrons consequently got drunk very quickly, spilling out onto the streets even faster than their money rolled into the state's coffers. Moreover, adulterated vodka remained widely available. The Guardianship became a magnet of criticism. In particular, civil Temperance workers found the state's calls for moderation hypocritical and insincere, given its vested interest in selling vodka.

In 1894 Tsar Nicholas II (1868–1917) assumed the throne. Like his father, he believed that something drastic had to be done about Russia's persistent drinking problem. But he too failed to curb abuse. In 1904–5, during the disastrous Russo–Japanese War, recruits routinely showed up inebriated and drunken sailors and soldiers were said to have contributed to Russia's shocking defeats at Port Arthur and the Battle of

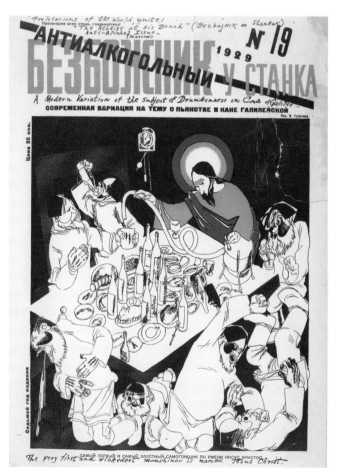

Jesus as moonshiner. In 1929 the atheist magazine *The Godless* attacked both the Orthodox Church and moonshiners by depicting Christ at Cana transforming water into vodka.

Mukden. On the eve of the First World War, determined to eradicate the problem once and for all, and no doubt emboldened by the continued demands on the part of temperance societies, he banned vodka for the duration of the war.

Unfortunately for the Tsar, the move backfired. As a result of the ban, and just when Russia sorely needed money to finance the war, nearly a third of its revenues evaporated. Some soldiers went to the front without boots or rifles. Worse, domestic consumption of vodka did not abate. The surplus grain, which normally would have been transported to the large cities, piled up in villages because most trains were reserved for troop movements. Local peasants thus had an ample supply from which they produced moonshine (*samogon*).

As the war dragged on, illegal vodka production increased. Consequently many urban centres far removed from the supply of grain, including the capital, St Petersburg, ran out of bread and flour. In February 1917 women protesting the shortages of flour sparked the first phase of the revolution that ultimately forced the Tsar to abdicate. Eight months later, the Bolsheviks seized power.

6
The Soviets and Vodka

The new Marxist leaders of Russia, who blamed drunkenness on capitalism, initially insisted that sobriety would reign in their new socialist society. They imposed their own total ban on vodka, with even stricter penalties than those of the Tsar, to ensure that the Red Army had a sufficient supply of grain during Russia's bloody Civil War. Indeed, if caught, moonshiners were likely to face a firing squad. Still, some peasants boldly persisted in the production of *samogon*.

In the early 1920s, once Lenin had consolidated power, the Soviet Union gradually reintroduced low-grade alcoholic drinks on the state-controlled market. Finally, in October 1925, full-strength vodka became legal once again. But the reacceptance of alcoholic beverages was motivated by pragmatic considerations, rather than a shift in ideology. The Bolshevik state, bankrupted by a costly four-year world war and a devastating two-year civil war, and nearly entirely ostracized from the world market, desperately needed to raise revenues to rebuild its ravaged economy.

In 1930 the new leader Joseph Stalin ordered the state to step up its vodka production. Like his predecessors, the tsars, he fully appreciated the revenue-generating potential of the potent libation, even if increased distribution and availability

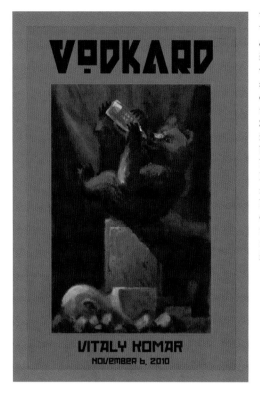

VODKARD

VITALY KOMAR
NOVEMBER 6, 2010

Vitaly Komar's Vodkard ('vodka card'). In this image by a well-known and formerly dissident artist, the fall of the Soviet regime is symbolized by the toppled bust. The Russian people, represented by the cub, celebrate their newfound freedom by imbibing vodka.

inevitably led to greater rate of alcoholism among the population. Stalin argued: 'What is better, being in bondage to foreign capital or to vodka revenue?'

With a treasury replenished with vodka profits, Stalin then launched a massive industrialization project billed as the first Five Year Plan. At about the same time, he banned all Temperance societies. Indeed Stalin, a hearty imbiber himself and an inveterate night owl, had little sympathy for their cause. He frequently hosted lavish late-night dinner parties at the Kremlin, as well as less formal get-togethers at his dachas, which were, by all accounts, awash with vodka.

Like Peter the Great, Stalin also used vodka as a political tool. At his dinners, which often doubled as policy meetings, he gave long toasts to his loyal followers and used the liquid to solidify friendships. At the same time, he plied the less trustworthy at his table with vodka to suppress their inhibitions so that he could extract valuable information. Although some historians maintain that Stalin himself occasionally drank to excess, most of his contemporaries agreed that he was a measured drinker, at least when surrounded by company. Perhaps his most famous toast was the one he delivered at the close of the Second World War, dedicated 'to the Russian people'. Ostensibly it served to celebrate Hitler's death and victory over the Nazis, but many believe it quietly signalled his intent to persecute Jews, who were widely viewed as not genuinely Russian.

After Stalin's death in 1953 alcoholism in the Soviet Union continued to rise. A few state-sponsored Temperance societies were organized from time to time, with little effect. The British writer Colin Thubron, who drove across the Soviet Union in the early 1980s, described the role of vodka ('that colourless innocence!') in his book *Where Nights Are Longest* (1983):

> It's the curse and liberation of Russia, a self-obliterating escape from tedium and emptiness, from interminable winter nights, and the still longer darker nights of the soul. It is drunk in furious, catatonic debauches, with the full intention of rendering its drinkers virtually insensible. Bottles are always tipped dry, glasses drained at a gulp.

Not until Mikhail Gorbachev became General Secretary of the Communist Party in 1985 did the regime take drastic steps to fight the growing problem. His first official measure, in fact, was to enact laws to suppress public drunkenness. Borrowing a page from Nicholas II's playbook, he created the

When Mikhail Gorbachev came to power in 1985, he attempted to curb vodka consumption by limiting the hours when vodka could be sold, creating huge queues at liquor stores.

Volunteer Temperance Society. Like its tsarist predecessor, it was supposed to plan wholesome outings and musical entertainment for the masses, to elevate their cultural appreciation while educating them about the evils of alcohol abuse. But this organization was on a far grander scale than its predecessor. In fact, with some 114 million members – virtually the entire adult population of the Soviet Union – membership was hardly voluntary. Gorbachev ordered the society's bureaucrats to set up chapters in every factory, university, government department and other institutions. Meanwhile, to ensure that the public did not migrate to other alcoholic drinks (such as wine), he had entire vineyards uprooted. He decreed that official events be vodka-free, and he severely limited the hours of sale at state liquor stores.

Gorbachev's alcohol policy was entirely consistent with his celebrated *perestroika* or restructuring of society. He wanted

Russian Temperance poster, 'Nyet'. This iconic Soviet anti-alcohol poster from the 1950s, showing a clean-cut Russian resolutely refusing a glass of vodka, represents an early variation of the 'just say no' imperative.

Soviet Temperance poster with the snake, a traditional symbol of alcoholism, crawling up the left side of the bottle with the heading 'the destruction of hope'.

a healthier population to make the Soviet Union more productive. And to some extent he succeeded. According to some defenders, his campaign saved nearly a million lives while raising life expectancies. So great was the public backlash, however, that he had to beat a hasty retreat a mere two years into his ambitious campaign. His popularity plummeted to such an extent that few Soviets lamented his fall from power in 1991. Like Nicholas II, his bold bid to reform time-honoured Russian drinking habits fizzled and seems to have contributed to a premature political demise. Is it any wonder that Russia's current rulers are wary of Temperance programmes?

In fact, throughout Eastern Europe vodka, as in the nineteenth century, remains a form of social glue. In his book *Belarus* (2008), Nigel Roberts described drinking habits in Russia's Slavic neighbour.

> Every holiday, birthday, wedding, christening and funeral is celebrated with traditional toasts of vodka. Business deals are sealed with a vodka flourish. Family events and social gatherings, particularly to welcome new friends and visitors would be unthinkable without a half-litre bottle on the table with plenty more in reserve should (when!) the need arise. I have drunk with the Metropolitan Filaret of All Belarus, with a state lawyer at 09.30 (in his office) to celebrate his birthday, with a headmaster in his office during the school day, at breakfast with the father of my host family, and by night on a farm near to a roaring fire with rural elders gathered around, singing songs and exchanging stories. Toast after toast.

Slavs – and even resident non-abstemious Muslims – are deeply offended if a guest refuses a drink, as they interpret that refusal as a rejection of their hospitality and friendship.

Recently, an American missionary couple lamented that, after living in the Caucasus for ten years, they had failed to convert a single Muslim. Perhaps they had neglected to exchange shots of vodka with the locals. The Soviet dissident writer A. Tertz (Andrew Sinyasky) attempted to explain Russian drinking as the seeking of a religious experience:

> The Russian people drink not from need and not from grief, but from an age-old requirement for the miraculous and extraordinary. Drink if you will mystically, striving to transport the soul beyond earth's gravity and return it to its sacred incorporeal state. Vodka is the Russian *muzhik*'s (peasant) White Magic. He decidedly prefers it to Black Magic, the female.

Perhaps the ultimate literary homage from Soviet Russia to vodka is *Moscow to the End of the Line* by Venedikt Erofeev. This hilarious and hallucinatory paean from the 1960s celebrates the glories and indignities of inebriation under Soviet rule. The narrator is an intelligent and educated alcoholic, presumably the author himself, who is riding the subway en route to the end of the line where he intends to greet his sweetheart and child with flowers and candy. As his hankering for alcohol overtakes him, however, he is forced to make innumerable detours to satisfy his cravings. He is finally reduced to consuming denatured spirits, eau-de-cologne, varnish and even shoe polish. Along the way, he banters with his fellow travellers on life, love, religion, literature and philosophy.

Not until 1989, after the book had been circulating abroad for years, did the Soviet Union allow publication of an expurgated version. The full text, however, was not published in Russia until 1995, after the collapse of the Soviet Union. Indeed, more than a denunciation of alcohol, Erofeev's book

Russian anti-alcohol poster of the 1920s, reading: 'Stop. This is the final warning.'

СТ Й

ПОСЛЕДНЕЕ ПРЕДУПРЕЖДЕНИЕ

delivered a bitter and wry critique of Brezhnev's grey and stagnant Soviet Union where talent found no outlet beyond drinking. Funny and tragic, this book perfectly epitomizes its era. In 1998 a bronze monument to the author was erected in Red Square to commemorate his sixtieth birthday.

7
Vodka Invades the United States

The United States has long been the second greatest consumer of vodka, after Russia. Yet only a century ago, the American market for vodka was still relatively modest, centring on cheap varieties sold to the burgeoning population of Eastern European immigrants. Following the end of Prohibition in 1933, Rudolph Kunett, a Russian-born émigré, attempted to introduce higher-grade vodka under the famous Smirnoff label, the favourite of the imperial court of tsarist Russia. Kunett purchased the rights to the name and the company's groundbreaking charcoal-filtration method from Vladimir Smirnov. A son of the founder, Smirnov had settled in France after fleeing the revolution of 1917, where he had created Ste. Pierre Smirnoff Fils, before changing the spelling of the family name.

Kunett, himself a refugee from the Revolution, began a small distillery in Bethel, Connecticut. Business was poor, however. At first, only about 6,000 cases of vodka were sold annually in the USA. In 1939 John G. Martin, the English-born chairman of Heublein's liquor company in nearby Hartford, Connecticut, bought the distillery and its equipment for $14,000. According to the terms Kunett was to be retained as a supervisor for ten years and paid a royalty of 5 per cent on each bottle of Smirnoff sold.

Under Heublein's management sales remained flat, although one out-of-state distributor managed to ratchet up sales by advertising the new beverage as 'Smirnoff White Whiskey – No Smell, No Taste'. When Heublein folded into the British giant spirits company Diageo, Martin retained the rights to the Smirnoff name, still hoping to establish the brand in the USA.

In 1941 Martin visited a friend in Los Angeles, Jack Moran, who owned the Cock 'n' Bull Tavern. After it emerged that Moran had an oversupply of ginger beer, and Martin a large stock of unsold vodka, the two men discussed how they might combine their resources. They concocted a drink consisting

Smirnoff Vodka. The original company, founded in Moscow in the 1860s by Pyotr A. Smirnov, catered to the royal family. Now owned by the British company Diageo, it is one of the most widely sold vodkas in the world.

of vodka, ginger beer and fresh lime or lemon juice served in a copper mug. Billed as Moscow Mule (a drink with a kick), it sparked the first modest American demand for vodka.

After the war, however, growing anti-Soviet sentiment threatened to reverse vodka's gains. In the early 1950s bartenders paraded down New York's Fifth Avenue bearing the banner, 'Down with the Moscow Mule – We Don't Need Smirnoff Vodka.' The House of Seagram concluded that the American market was stagnant. It offered free vodka drinks for an entire week to conventioneers in Los Angeles, only to find no takers. The disgusted president of the company, General Frank Schwengel, allegedly picked up the entire case of vodka and flung it into the hotel swimming pool, and was heard muttering: 'So much for the future of vodka in America.'

Fortunately for Martin, the negative publicity actually seems to have boosted demand for Moscow Mule. His spirits buoyed, the entrepreneur introduced a steady stream of vodka concoctions, using tea, beef bouillon, orange juice and other flavourings. He also pioneered a now familiar marketing ploy: running magazine advertisements featuring famous people in exotic places enjoying vodka cocktails.

Still, the domestic flow of vodka remained but a trickle until 1962, when *Dr No*, the first James Bond film, reached theatres nationwide. Sean Connery orders a Martini made with Smirnoff vodka, and first uttered the famous words, 'shaken, not stirred'. Suddenly, vodka demand spiked.

But the real breakthrough for American vodka sales took place a decade later, when Richard Nixon visited the Soviet Union to ease tensions, in accordance with his policy of détente. The President subsequently authorized his good friend Donald Kendall, the Chief Executive Officer of Pepsi-Cola, to do business with the Soviets. The American company agreed to help the Soviet government set up a factory with

James Bond (Sean Connery) prepares a Martini. In the 1962 movie *Dr No* Bond utters the famous line, 'shaken, not stirred', as he introduces American viewers to a Smirnoff Martini.

the capacity to produce 74 million bottles of cola a year, using Pepsi's syrup. The cash-strapped Soviets were allowed to pay in vodka.

PepsiCo, in effect, became the sole American agents for the popular Soviet-produced Stolichnaya Vodka, known widely simply as 'Stoli', to be distributed through a subsidiary with the odd name Monsieur Henri Wines. Sales exploded. In 1975, for the first time in history, American vodka surpassed bourbon to become the leading national liquor, claiming 18.7 per cent of the market. The Soviet Union likewise profited from the deal. By 1990, when the empire was beginning to crumble, it was producing 40 million cases of cola in 26 factories. The government even struck a deal with Pepsi-Cola to open 24 more cola plants. The American firm, in return, upped its demand for Stolichnaya and also agreed to buy or lease at least ten Soviet-built freighters and tankers, mostly to be sold as scrap metal.

This prodigious exchange of liquids was an odd arrangement indeed. To detractors of both beverages, the two countries were merely swapping their own varieties of chilled poison. The arrangement was particularly amusing to the Russians, who had branded Americans 'Coca-Cola fascists' during the Cold War, and had accused them of the 'Coca-Colonization'

A Martini glass: the classic shape of the now omnipresent vodka and dry vermouth cocktail.

Fathulla Shakirov, Stolichnaya Vodka advertisement, 1998. One of several designed by the Tashkent-born artist, this poster evokes a pseudo avant-garde style as it proclaims, 'There has never been better.'

of the world. Even today, the deal still evokes smiles in Russia. In 2009 a clever publisher issued a calendar comprised of a collection of doctored Soviet anti-alcohol posters, with Coca-Cola bottles taking the place of the original vodka bottles.

8

Brands, Bottles and Boutiques:
Vodka Diversifies

Most varieties of spirits – including gin, bourbon, rye, Scotch, cognac and numerous liqueurs – have their own distinctive taste, even within their own category. Branding is therefore strongly associated with the liquor's unique taste, while the use of familiar bottles and labels merely underscores a sense of tradition and guaranteed quality.

Vodka, however, often lacks a distinctive taste, so its branding is almost entirely in the packaging. It is rumoured, in fact, that one variety, known as 'railway car vodka', is shipped to several different liquor companies, where it is bottled under multiple brands and sold at different price points. If it were true, this practice would of course have to be a closely guarded secret, because the public would naturally buy only the cheapest variety if it realized that all these brands are in fact identical.

Vodka is a postmodern drink: distillers must find creative ways to 'construct' their branding, projecting real or imaginary qualities through their packaging. And the purchaser, by choosing one brand over another, effectively labels himself. Adam Rosen, the brand manager of Wyborowa Vodka, affirms this dichotomy:

approved by Mikhail T. Kalashnikov, designer of the AK-47 rifle. It was the first vodka ever to be created by combining salt, sugar, vanillin and glycerine.' At least the publicist did not proclaim it to be a blast. Russia also produces four-times distilled and nine-times filtered Red Army Vodka in a bottle in the shape of a bomb. Poland's Military 5 Vodka is also shaped like a bomb. Continuing the military theme is the Armenian Elite's vodka bottle, shaped like a sword in a scabbard. Moldova produces a honey vodka aptly called Firestarter in the shape of a fire extinguisher, complete with a locking pin, trigger and nozzle through which vodka is dispensed.

Poland offers Jazz Vodka bottled in a whimsical trumpet-shape. Not surprisingly the USA produces Gotham Vodka, in a porcelain skyscraper-shaped bottle, while Russia's Standard manufactures Le Eiffel Vodka in a bottle to

Kalashnikov Vodka in a case. The bottle is shaped as the famous AK-47 assault rifle designed by Mikhail Kalashnikov. The former Soviet general personally endorses the product, vaunted for its 'military strength' (42 per cent alcohol instead of the usual 40 per cent).

match its name. Pacesetter Vodka can be found in a ceramic John Deere green-and-yellow tractor-shaped bottle. Russia's Gzhel Vodka comes in whimsical animal shapes of blue and white pottery. Johnson's Vodka can be found in a beautiful coloured ceramic bottle in the form of a sparrowhawk. Vodka also can be procured in standard aluminium drinks cans, which are not considered collectibles by most; perhaps consumers just find them convenient. Also geared for convenience, not elegance, are the plastic four-ounce (120 ml) containers of vodka with rip-off aluminium foil lids.

For the wealthy who are willing to pay up to $2,000, there is the Imperial Vodka Collection. The 750-millilitre bottle is shaped like the classic Fabergé Easter egg of metal alloy covered in enamel and decorated with gilded elements

Firestarter Vodka.

plated with 18-carat gold; the carafe is made of Venetian glass also with 18-carat décor. The set is completed with four crystal and gold shot cups. The special quality of the vodka is attributed to the minerals in the water and its purification through highly active birch charcoal and a platinum filter. No doubt Russo-Baltique Vodka – a brand the automobile manufacturer Dartz created in 2009 to mark its hundreth anniversary – is the most expensive in the world: a bottle retails at £790,000 (9.8 million rubles). The bottle is a replica of the radiator guard of the Prombron Monaco Red Diamond Edition, a car selling for the equivalent of £1 million (12.4 million rubles). This suv has gold-plated windows, pure tungsten exhausts, instrument gauges encrusted with diamonds and seats covered with whale-penis leather. The purchaser of this car will receive three bottles of Russo-Baltique Vodka. The radiator-guard-reproduction bottle is made from gold coins minted between 1908 and 1912, the era when the car was first produced. The cap of the bottle is made of white and yellow gold and contains a diamond-encrusted replica of the Russian Imperial Eagle. The bottle itself is made of bulletproof glass, appropriate enough to accompany the armoured car. The producer rather gratuitously adds that the vodka is not meant to be drunk, as the bottle itself is suitable to be displayed as a work of art.

Germany's new premium vodka Vallure, in gold-plated bottles, will retail at about a million dollars per bottle. Le Billionaire, as the name suggests, is for people with butlers. The label is encrusted with many diamonds, gold and Swarovski crystals. The $3.7-million, three-litre bottle also comes with a diamond-covered faux fur cover and white gloves for the butler.

Crystal Head vodka, in a skull-shaped bottle, is not meant to suggest the imminent demise of the consumer, but refers to a legend that thirteen crystal heads have been unearthed from the Yucatan to Tibet at various times. Supposedly, the skulls emit positive energy, good will and prosperity – properties the manufacturers would like the purchaser to associate with Crystal Head, which is triple-filtered through polished crystals known as Herkimer diamonds so that the result is a pure 'spirit', free of adulterants. This vodka is clearly playing on the film *Indiana Jones and the Kingdom of the Crystal Skull* (2008). Dan Aykroyd, the Canadian actor, TV personality and screenwriter with a strong belief in spiritualism, conceived the idea of this particular vodka, and travels widely to promote the $50 bottle.

Labels should either be gorgeous or intriguing. In the latter category is Death's Door, which appears to appeal to the daring. But some labels are deceptive. Death's Door refers to a strait between Green Bay, Wisconsin and Lake Michigan where Washington Island sits. There the makers of Death's Door grow organic wheat (no herbicides or pesticides) from which they distil vodka in small batches. The intended message therefore is to suggest that the drink is wholesome and friendly to the environment and not that the imbiber will find himself at death's door!

It's not just the bottle and label that need to be alluring; certain vodkas also pitch themselves at specific audiences. Absolut Vodka Company, in June 2009, agreed to sponsor programming for 'Gay Pride' month on the networks IFC and Sundance. Diageo is also courting the gay community by promoting its Ketel One at New York's Love Ball, attended by 2,000 gays and lesbians and featuring drag queens, a fête that can be viewed from the street via giant TVs. They also sponsored Pride Week parties in New York and San Francisco as well as 'mover and shaker' events at various New York nightclubs. Several other sources report that vodka is a preferred drink

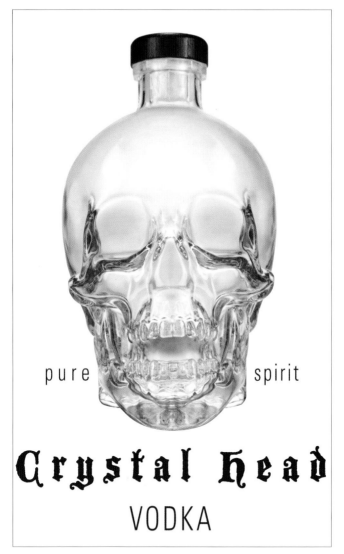

pure   spirit

Crystal Head

VODKA

Crystal Head Vodka. A Canadian premium vodka in a skull-shaped bottle to suggest spiritual power and enlightenment.

Death's Door Vodka. Named for a water passage between Washington Island and the Door County Peninsula in Wisconsin, this brand prides itself on its eco-friendly product and practices. It uses organic wheat, recycles water and distributes its spent mash to local hog and dairy farms.

among the gay community, partly because it is perceived as less fattening than other alcoholic beverages. Targeting the gay community pays off, since market research has estimated that the purchasing power of American lesbians and gays will exceed $835 billion in 2011.

Typical of one consumer was his remark that he chooses vodka as a preferred alcoholic drink when on a diet because the lighter the colour of the drink, the fewer the calories. Perhaps for the same reason, vodka appeals to young drinkers, especially women. Smirnoff advertises its 35 per cent alcohol Twist of Black Cherry Pre-Mix as having only 69 calories per ounce (30 ml) and includes a discussion of healthy alternative vodka choices, such as their vodka for thirteen fewer calories and Smirnoff Mojito Vodka with eleven fewer calories. Voli Vodka claims to be the first low-calorie vodka, but it achieves this at the expense of reducing the alcoholic content to 30 per cent, thus technically disqualifying it from being classified as a vodka.

Analysts of the trade claim that flavoured vodkas have succeeded partly because they have broadened vodka sales to

Ketel One Vodka. Launched in the Netherlands in the 17th century, this brand is named after the copper pot stills originally used in distillation. Now owned by Diageo, the company is famous for its ads proclaiming, 'Gentlemen, This is Vodka.'

women. Certainly, in 2009 the model and actress Elizabeth Hurley made it clear she was dropping wine and coffee from her diet in order to maintain a flat stomach and had turned to vodka with fizzy water and lime juice as her drink of choice, although she admitted it tasted like medicine to her at first. Another star, Jennifer Aniston, was quoted as saying, 'Vodka's what I drink. That's my drink of choice actually. It's a clean, um, liquor, yes. You know, no sugar.'

Distillers are indeed attempting to seduce women into drinking 'feminine' vodka, such as Damskaya, manufactured by Deyros, a Russian company. A lavender feminine-shaped bottle draped in a billowing skirt, suggestive of Marilyn Monroe, bears the inscription in Russian, 'between us women'. Damskaya is supposed to appeal to working women who can afford $12 a bottle of 40 per cent alcohol to be had in five flavours including lime, vanilla and almond. Will this be the drink of choice at career women's hen parties? Clearly the manufacturer hopes so. Some users of Smirnoff Vodka in Spain have formed a chat room in which they dress up their avatars, decorate their rooms and chat about their interests, an activity that suggests the participation of young female drinkers.

On the other hand, if you are a young and trendy single male, your choice might well be Svedka, whose advertising persona is a robot with prominent breasts, hips and thong-clad rear. The Svedka robot, or cyborg – half robot, half woman – is sometimes described as having 'a mechanical dominatrix look'. To lure those who consider themselves to be ahead of the pack, the ads proclaim 'Voted No. 1 in 2033'. To emphasize the brand as one for young clubbers, the bottle has been redesigned to resemble a tapered body, with the brand name Svedka standing out against a vibrant, coloured background. Even more explicitly sexual is the packaging of Sexy Tina Milky Vodka, consisting of vodka and Irish cream liquor in a container shaped like a breast. The makers hope to appeal to bachelors and women who wish to purchase provocative gifts for their male friends. Ketel One has also put out an ad designed to make men drinking their vodka feel macho. Part of it runs, 'There was a time when men were men. It was last night. Inspired by 300 years of tradition, Ketel One. Gentlemen, this is vodka.'

To reach the African-American market, various brands sponsor music festivals featuring jazz, hip-hop or other modern music. One example comes from the British firm Diageo, which sponsored a Fourth of July holiday weekend music festival featuring DJ Biz Markie and Salt-N-Pepa, explaining that the black community is important to sales. For lovers of rock music, there is the 2009 limited edition of Absolut's Rock bottle wrapped in a case of leather and studs, which 'pays tribute to the vibrant, bold and irreverent world of rock'.

While in the US African Americans make up a minority of the population, Hispanics, according to the United States Census Bureau, constituted 38 per cent of the under-eighteen population in 2000 and are increasing four times faster than the white population, thus providing a critical mass of drinkers of legal age. To target the Hispanic community, or 'cluster group', Diageo, the company that owns Ketel One, is using Spanish-language bus shelter ads and merchandise to promote its Yankees baseball team sponsorship. Diageo also runs Spanish radio ads in California, while in Chicago they fund scholarships for Hispanics in the hospitality industry.

A very particular niche market is that of dog lovers. In 2007 Melissa Zeppa and Kerry Schmelzer began to produce Black Lab Vodka to celebrate the American couple's favourite breed of dog, black labrador retrievers. Zeppa, an artist, designed the bottle, which features the eponymous dog on the label. In addition, a micro-handcraft vodka distillery in Oregon produces Dog Style Vodka, with an etching of Winston, the family pet bulldog pup, on the French-glass bottle.

Politicians also appeal to their constituencies by promoting brands of vodka in their own name. For example, during the 1996 presidential election in Russia, the ultranationalist candidate Vladimir Zhirinovsky raised funds and publicized his name by selling vodka with his name and his picture on the label. He lost. The winner of the presidential election in 1996 was Boris Yeltsin who, according to former US President Bill Clinton, got so drunk during a visit to Washington that he was

Black Lab Vodka. An example of the many artisanal vodkas that cater to niche markets, this super-premium American vodka comes in beautiful crystal bottles.

found standing outside the White House in his underpants trying to hail a cab to go and buy a pizza. The following night he was mistaken for a drunken intruder when he was discovered stumbling around the basement of his guesthouse by Secret Service agents. Despite Vladimir Putin's apparent disapproval of vodka (he prefers beer), on 1 November 2003 Moscow Distillery Cristall produced a new limited edition vodka called Putinka after Vladimir Putin. The drink is described as 'a luxurious drink for having joy, opening out, overcoming fatigue and relaxing'. It is now the second most popular brand in Russia. A vodka called Volodya i Medvedi, meaning Volodya and the Bears, a play on President Dmitry Medvedev's last name (which means bear) and the diminutive for Putin's first name, is now made in Ukraine and exported to Russia because the Russian Registry Office refused to grant a patent to this label. Clearly, Putin and Medvedev do not want their names lent to yet another vodka. A more disturbing brand is the Russian Civil Defence (*Grazhdanskya Oborona*), whose label displays a worker taken from a Nazi poster that once urged Germans to vote for Hitler. Presumably this brand is intended to appeal to ultranationalists and racists.

In 2004 Hillary Clinton reportedly challenged John McCain, then a colleague in the Senate, to a vodka-drinking contest while both were in Estonia on a Congressional tour. Senator Clinton, it seems, won the contest, at which point McCain proclaimed her 'one of the guys'. Bill Clinton was also spotted drinking vodka with Prime Minister Vladimir Putin at the Davos Conference of 2008. That same year, Svedka vodka offered presidential candidates Hillary Clinton, Barack Obama and McCain free vodka throughout Election Day, to 'put the party back into party politics', though none accepted the offer. In 2009 Glenn Kroll, a candidate for district attorney in the state of New York, took advantage of the similarity of his last name with the Polish vodka Krol by handing out bottles of the vodka affixed with campaign stickers to potential voters, a tactic many protested as tantamount to bribery.

For nearly three decades Absolut has issued print advertisements featuring cities, and it has also singled out four cities for which it put forth special vodkas. The latest is a limited edition of 60,000 bottles of Absolut Vancouver. The label, created by the award-winning Victoria-based illustrator and graphic designer Douglas Fraser, shows a yellow and blue seaplane soaring above the Vancouver skyline. A contest among local artists resulted in a $120,000 commission to create an artwork, series or educational programme that would be a gift to the city with some of the profits from sales going to the arts. The Boston edition, flavoured with black tea and elderflower with a green label, was designed to honour the Green Monster, the name of the large wall in Boston's Fenway Baseball Park. The vodka company donates part of its profits to a worthy cause. In the case of Boston, the company gave $50,000 to the local Charles River Conservancy. An earlier edition was Absolut Los Angeles, flavoured with blueberry, acai berry, acerola cherry and pomegranate. The company gave $250,000 from the sale of their special edition to Green Way Los Angeles. In 2007, to mark the second anniversary of the disastrous hurricane Katrina, Absolut produced 35,000 cases of New Orleans vodka, flavoured with mango and black pepper, with the entire two million dollars or so in sales going to Gulf State Charity. Tru Organic Vodka also supports a New Orleans charity, the restoration of Lake Pontchartrain's New Canal Lighthouse. For every bottle sold in the area, the vodka company donates a dollar to the cause.

A good example of a company that touts its anti-fancy bottle and anti-hype in advertising is Polish Sobieski Vodka. In 2007 its 'Truth in Vodka' marketing campaign urged consumers to focus on the bottle's contents, rather than on gimmicky marketing techniques and overpriced packaging. This back-to-basics campaign helped Sobieski Vodka, which is made from Dankowski rye at the Starogard Gdanski distillery, dating back to 1846, to break the sales record for a newly introduced spirit. In 2008 255,000 cases of Sobieski were sold in the US in the first full calendar year. They hope soon to reach the one-million-case sales milestone.

Celebrities are now making their own brands of vodka. The company Louis Vuitton launched two new Belvedere vodka brands. Justin Timberlake's own brand is hot peppered vodka. A small artisanal company in Idaho produced a corn and rye vodka, featuring pomegranate and habanero pepper flavours, labelled Hendrix Electric Vodka, named of course after Jimi Hendrix. Not only do celebrities own substantial shares in vodka companies, but many stars endorse a particular brand, earning a considerable sum. In an old Woody Allen sketch, he receives a phone call from someone offering him an opportunity to endorse a vodka company: 'No,' Allen replies. 'I'm an artist. I do not do commercials. I don't pander. I don't drink vodka and if I did, I certainly would not drink your product.' The vodka salesman then mentions the enormous payment he would receive, to which the comedian responds, 'Hold on. I'll put Mr Allen on the phone.'

As well as celebrities, freewheeling entrepeneurs have also been known to make their own brands of vodka – such as Bob Popplewell, who raises reptiles on his Texas ranch. He got into trouble with the law, however, when he began to market his bottles of homemade vodka that contained dead baby rattlesnakes. He defended himself by saying that the bottles were marked 'not for human consumption', but he also noted, 'Some Asian cultures use this snake concoction for energy that keeps you going all night.' We are reminded of the old Polish vodka infused with adders, mentioned earlier. Beating off intense competition, the first African American to own a vodka company was former recording artist, real estate mogul and sports agent Victor G. Harvey, who launched his V. Georgio Vodka with several glittering parties in Miami, Florida, in 2009. Explaining why he turned to making vodka, he said that it 'could transcend all different barriers and all different walks of life'. In 2008 Russian Standard Vodka sponsored a two-week tour of nine American cities with Miss Russia contestants. In 2007 Roustam Tariko, the founder of Standard, invited Martha Stewart, the American TV personality and food authority, for a tour of Moscow and St Petersburg, where he hosted and toasted her with his own vodka at a lavish dinner in the former Imperial Grand Duke Vladimir Palace.

At times labels are meant to suggest playfulness, entertainment and the possibility of constructing a new identity. For example, for a limited period from 2008 through to January 2009 Absolut Vodka displayed special gift-packs in various airport duty-free shops with the tagline, 'In an Absolut World Every Night is a Masquerade.' This was to showcase a glamorous new Absolut bottle, Masquerade, covered by a jacket of exactly 3,238 shiny red sequins that zipped off on the back. 'Absolut is taking masquerade into the modern era where the possibilities of being yourself and expressing your personality are more important than ever.' In short, labels can liberate and bottles can fascinate.

For those who are allergic to gluten, there is a website for gluten-free vodka.

One of the target markets is kosher vodka for Orthodox Jews or others who wish to drink kosher. All US non-flavoured domestic vodka made of grain or potato is acceptable. Stolichnaya Vodka (meaning capital city), reputedly the best-selling Russian vodka in the USA, was the first major vodka brand to be certified kosher by the Orthodox Union, an event that occurred in 1996. Canadian Crystal Head Vodka has also been certified as kosher. Kashrut.com provides a list of approved imported vodkas. Kosher vodka has acquired the reputation of causing little or no hangover. According to *The Penguin Book of Spirits and Liqueurs*, vodka's

> low level of fusel oils and congenerics – impurities that flavour spirits but that can contribute to the after-effects of heavy consumption – led to its being considered among the 'safer' spirits, though not in terms of its powers of intoxication, which, depending on strength, may be considerable.

An example of a vodka designed for Jewish consumption is the Russian-produced Obetovannaya Vodka (Promised Vodka) whose label, bottle and packaging are designed to suggest references to the Promised Land. The Russian Urozhai distillery located near Moscow produces Yevreskaya Vodka (Jewish Vodka) under rabbinical supervision. Yevreskaya features its rabbinical approval and 'Jewish content' as part of its marketing strategy. The black labels are laden with Jewish symbols and imagery – Hebrew letters, a menorah, a photo of the interior of the Moscow Choral Synagogue and a photo of an Orthodox rabbi and a Jew in a white yarmulke standing next to the portrait of the late Lubavitcher Rebbe, Menachem Mendel Schneerson. Other kosher vodkas are produced by a distillery in Birobidzhan, which Stalin declared an autonomous Jewish region in 1934, but none sells as well as Yevreskaya.

An Israeli distillery produces L'Chaim Kosher Vodka. According to author Lucy M. Long, there are 30 more brands of kosher vodka circulating in Poland. Some labels show alluring Jewish women such as Rachela Vodka, others show Orthodox males with traditional hats such as Cymes Vodka. Perhaps the most successful kosher vodka in Poland is Nisskosher. A Polish Jewish distiller distils it in Germany along with philanthropist Sigmund Nissenbaum, who as chairman of the Nissenbaum Foundation has restored hundreds of Polish Jewish cemeteries, synagogues and other cultural sites to their original states. Vodka Perfect is the largest kosher vodka manufacturer in Eastern Europe and the biggest vodka producer in Israel. It uses Galilee water and offers the possibility of selling kosher vodka to individuals who can affix their own private label to the bottles.

Kosher vodka labels. These labels are designed to appeal to observant Jews, while evoking the motif of vodka and romance.

In another marketing ploy, Absolut Vodka has issued numbered limited-edition bottles with no label or logo. A discreet and easily removable sticker with a campaign manifesto encourages consumers to discard their prejudices and labels and look beyond the obvious. A spokesperson for Absolut, Anders Olsson, announced, 'For the first time, we're facing the world stark naked. We're launching a bottle with no label and no logo, to manifest the idea that no matter what's on the outside, it's the inside that really matters. We do it in support of the people who spend their entire lives branded with labels by others.' At last it would appear that a vodka brand is representing itself as having universal appeal to all.

L'Chaim Kosher Vodka. An Israeli brand meaning 'to life', it aspires to appeal to 'all people from everywhere regardless of social, political, cultural, economic or religious backgrounds'.

The no-label project was intended to remove the distinctiveness of the brand and yet, by presenting a no-label bottle, no vodka company could be more distinct.

It would appear, however, that the manufacturers of Absolut are no longer willing to rely entirely on bottle shapes, labels and advertising in the print media. In the summer of 2009 they launched a new form of promotion – the Drinkspiration, an application for iPod Touch and Android users. The device can recommend hundreds of different vividly illustrated vodka drinks using Absolut depending on the weather, time of day, venue and personal taste of the user. Thirteen days after Drinkinspiration first became available, Swedes had already downloaded recipes 43,000 times. In keeping with growing trend for letting the world know what one is doing and drinking, users can share their choices with their social networks through Facebook and Twitter. In the same vein, Tito's Handmade Vodka sponsors a free application for iPhone or iTouch, called Happy Hours, which identifies good prices in local bars. Users can add names of bars, photos and reviews of pub visits. One might ask whether a person can be texting, tweeting and drinking at the same time.

Perhaps the most significant innovation in the vodka business is the emergence and proliferation of small, artisanal vodka companies. As one vodka producer noted, 'Spirits are the next big artisanal farm product.' In 2003 there were only about 60 artisan distillers in the USA, but by 2009 that number increased to 160. Vodka craft distillers go to great lengths to distinguish themselves from assembly-line distilleries. The proliferation of these small vodka companies is truly astonishing, especially in the USA, where there is a tradition of individual entrepreneurship and a public constantly seeking novelty. Some seem to find sufficient purchasers to assure survival but many others fall by the wayside. One success story appears to be the aforementioned Tito's Handmade Vodka, created about a dozen years ago by Bert Butler 'Tito' Beveridge II, who first began his business as a hobby and distributed his product as gifts to his friends. The first distillery in Texas, his company has grown from a few bottles to over 200,000 cases a year, sold widely throughout the USA and Canada. He financed his original one-room distillery by using advances on eighteen credit cards. Consumers with whom he stays in contact through email promote the super-premium vodka by word of mouth. Unlike the larger international corporations (he now has just seventeen employees), Beveridge spends relatively little on the bottle, label or packaging of his prize-winning product. Made in small batches from 100 per cent organic white corn, the American Rain Vodka, first produced in 1996, is one of the earliest organic vodkas. Another, Bee Vodka, released by Hidden Marsh Distillery in New York State in 2008, is made with honey. Craft distiller Steve Viezbicke, 44, a Boulder native and founder of 303 Vodka, speaks of his passion for making vodka: 'For some reason it just gets in your blood. It's an art.' It is also a family tradition. He follows a recipe he found in an old steamer trunk that had been used by his Polish grandfather.

Quay, ultra-premium, artisan-crafted Mediterranean Vodka produced in France, which boasts of being four times filtered and five times distilled, was introduced in the spring of 2009. Easter Seals of America served this vodka at their thank-you parties for fundraisers. Another example of a small enterprise is that of Manhattan/Hamptons nightclub entrepreneur Charles Ferri, who introduced Star Vodka, named for one of his clubs, the Star Room. Ferri's vodka is gluten-free, made for him in the Cascade Mountains of Oregon. It is filtered through lava rock, and made in very small batches. Donnie Thibodeau, a potato farmer, and his brother Lee, a

The Black Queen Vodka. A super-premium vodka, this Belgian brand uses a crumbly sugar known as cassonade to attain a distinctive colour. The stunning bottle is decorated with gold leaf and packed in a lacquered case.

neurosurgeon, teamed with ski instructor Bob Harkins to produce Cold River Vodka, Maine's first super-premium vodka made in a pot still from their own potatoes and handled from potato seed to bottling. It takes seven kilograms of potatoes to make one 750-millilitre bottle of vodka. On their own farm near Vancouver, British Columbia, three Schramm brothers make small-batch vodka from organic potatoes, which they distil twice only in order to retain as much aroma and taste as possible. Vermont Spirits, another artisanal product, sells three brands: Vermont White, distilled from milk sugars; Vermont Gold, made of maple syrup and limited to one thousand cases a year; and Vintage Gold, made of maple sap.

Some craft distillers in the USA invite tourists for tastings and tours of the premises, some with the support of their states in a general effort to attract tourism – much as winery visits have boosted sales and tourism in California and breweries in Wisconsin and elsewhere. Long Island Spirits, Inc., makers of LiV Vodka, an ultra-premium artisanal vodka that is distilled in small batches entirely from potatoes, has a state

LiV Vodka. Made on Long Island, New York, this potato vodka is one of a growing number of hand-crafted American vodkas. As is the case with most wineries, the public is welcome to visit the distillery and sample the product.

ground, especially among young people and women, who tend to prefer clear spirits.

Super-premium labels, which are generally enjoyed neat and straight from the freezer, are expected to capture a growing market share worldwide. Currently, the US accounts for 61 per cent of premium and above vodka sales, while Russia accounts for 28 per cent, and Europe virtually the entire balance. In the near future, however, demand for quality vodka is expected to intensify in certain emerging markets, such as Brazil, Russia, India and China, not to mention Mexico, Thailand and South Africa.

10

Market Prospects

Although the demand for vodka is growing in developing countries, at present most vodka consumed in these countries is produced by domestic non-premium distillers. As the World Trade Organization lowers international tariff barriers and as populations become increasingly urbanized, some experts predict that many of these countries will dramatically increase importation of premium vodka.

India offers an interesting case study. Once virtually unknown in that land, vodka gained a toehold in the early 1990s. A friend of mine tells me an amusing anecdote about its introduction. During the collapse of the Soviet Union, Soviet embassy workers in Delhi were deprived of their salaries. Desperate for income, they attempted to sell their stashes of vodka to the locals, who had little cash to offer in exchange. The staff eventually took goats for payment and shipped the animals back to Russia on Aeroflot for slaughter. It seems these public servants not only turned a good profit, but sparked a modest demand in India for imported vodka, despite high government tariffs.

Initially, vodka appealed primarily to Indian women, who judged the white, odourless drink lighter and more agreeable than the dark whiskies and rums traditionally imbibed by men. In order to sell the drink to men as well, publicists had to stress that, despite its innocuous appearance, vodka is just as strong as whisky. Their campaign eventually succeeded. In 1999 Romanov Vodka (many non-Russian firms opt for Russian-sounding names) became the first Indian brand to sell in excess of 100,000 cases. Two years later, the government allowed foreign makers to establish distilleries in India, although it retained high tariffs on foreign brands.

In recent years, vodka consumption in India has skyrocketed. In one year alone (2006) Indian demand grew by a brisk 20 per cent. Overall, consumption quadrupled between 2004 and 2008, rising from 1.2 to 4.8 million cases. Sales are now approaching seven million cases and may reach nine million by 2014. Both domestic and foreign firms are thriving. Romanov now sells more than one million cases a year – ten times what it sold a decade ago. Yet foreign brands, made abroad or in India by licence, still account for 75 per cent of Indian consumption.

Even premium brands are starting to appear in India and prosper, such as Eristoff Vodka, first made in 1806 for a Georgian prince. Among the foreign distillers, Diageo markets Shark Tooth, a high-end vodka containing ginseng in one of its versions. The brand is also exported to Bangladesh, Nepal and Sri Lanka, and can even be found in Africa and the Middle East. Roberto Cavalli Vodka was introduced to the Indian market in late 2009. Bearing the name of the famous Florentine designer, it is the first vodka made in Italy and it is filtered through chips of marble from Carrara. It comes in a white glass bottle encircled by a snake and advertises that it is 'captivating, seductive and the quintessence of femininity'.

Indian distillers are also offering premium products and a greater selection. Romanov, which already produces a number of flavours such as green apple and passion fruit, has recently

Roberto Cavalli Vodka. Named after the famous Italian designer, with a bottle evoking the feminine form, this vodka is the first to be made entirely within Italy. It is an example of how vodka production is expanding even within countries that have tradition-ally favoured other types of alcoholic beverages.

introduced Red, billed as 'India's first multi-grain and multi-distilled vodka'. Bollywood actress Shilpa Shetty, who has been promoting the brand since 2006, helped to launch the new product, which aims to capture a 20 per cent share of domestic production. Another Indian brand, White Mischief, offers vanilla, chocolate and strawberry flavours.

Even Vijay Mallya, a flamboyant entrepreneur, has entered the mix. In 2008 he announced to students at the London Business School that he was setting up a plant to produce diet vodka, developed by his scientific research foundation in Bangalore. Claiming to have thought 'outside the bottle', he revealed that among the ingredients is a plant called garceni, which contains natural substances that break down sugar and fat cells within the digestive system. Whether it can truly keep

European vodka drinkers both happy and fit remains to be seen, since its introduction has been delayed while the company hashes out classification issues with the European Union.

In China vodka has found a receptive new market. Sales have been rising by about 14 per cent a year, and by 2021 Chinese consumption of vodka is expected to rival that of the US. Vodka is now almost as popular as *baijiu* (literally 'white alcohol'), a centuries-old potent libation made of rice, sorghum or other grains. In 2009 the Chinese consumed 497 million cases of vodka compared to 520 million cases of *baijiu*. Much of the vodka comes from abroad. Poland, for example, supplies Wyborowa, the second most popular brand there, and two more Polish brands, Zubrówka and Absolwent, are set to enter the market.

But no foreign firm has a greater interest in the Chinese market than the British giant Diageo. In addition to exporting

White Mischief. Distilled in India, this brand illustrates the growing domestic production of vodka in a developing country.

its Smirnoff Vodka (the world's leading brand, sold to 120 countries on six continents), it has introduced a new premium product called Shanghai White Vodka. It is distilled four times over a period of six months, using both Russian and Chinese techniques. Launched in Hong Kong with great fanfare in June 2009, the vodka is now produced in the southwest city of Chengdu Shui. The distillery, called Jing Fang, is reputedly the oldest in the world, dating to the fourteenth century. The frosted bottles, which retail between $60 and $100, are a work of art, combining chinoiserie patterns of cherry blossoms with art deco designs of old Shanghai in silver and blue.

In 2007 vodka sales grew by 13 per cent in Taiwan, so Russia must have deemed the time ripe to add Taiwan to the other 70 countries to which it exports its number one premium vodka, Standart, outselling its nearest competitor five to one. Standart's portfolio grew by 40 per cent in 2007, making it the fourth fastest growing spirits brand worldwide, with the goal

Shanghai White. Produced in China by the Diageo company in collaboration with local distillers, this product will enjoy a huge market if it can compete success-fully with another strong alcoholic beverage, the ancient and popular *baijiu*.

of entering the Brazilian, Chinese and Indian markets. In general vodka is only a small share of alcohol consumption in Asia, but it is growing, particularly among young adults. The sale of Absolwent Vodka has doubled over the last year in Japan, while Zubrówka is sold in Laos and Cambodia. In 2009 Pernod Ricard spent 20 million baht to open its first vodka bar, Absolut Parc, at Parc Paragon in Bangkok, to cater to a growing taste for vodka over whiskey among Thais, expanding the market that had generally consisted of foreigners or Thais educated abroad.

Russian Standart linked an increased demand for its high quality premium vodka in Uzbekistan to the increased spending power of Uzbek consumers. Founded as recently as 1998 in St Petersburg, and selling over two million cases of vodka a year, Russian Standart (Standard) claims to be the first and leading premium vodka brand in Russia, but it exports 80 per cent of its production to Europe, the Americas and Asia including Singapore, Malaysia, Indonesia, Thailand, Vietnam, Cambodia, Myanmar, Laos and the Philippines.

In the summer of 2009 Standart began an ad campaign in the UK called 'Meet the Russian Standard'. It included a contest with the winners enjoying an all expenses paid two-day trip to Moscow, featuring a tour of the city, a personal meeting with the contestants vying to become Miss Russia, luxury accommodations, fine dining in Moscow's most exclusive restaurants and of course vodka tastings, not to mention a shopping spree, a spa session and a personal makeover.

The Ukrainian vodka Nemiroff, promoted by Lady Gaga in the music video for her song 'Bad Romance', which was seen by over eight million viewers within days of its release, sells 45 per cent of its premium brand to Russia. Among the other 35 countries that import this brand are Canada, Australia and the US, as well as the biggest vodka-consuming countries of

Chinggis vodka. Produced in Mongolia and named after that nation's well-known conqueror, Genghis Khan, this exported prize-winning brand underscores how vodka is now truly a global product.

Europe, the Baltic States and the former Soviet Union: Kazakhstan, Azerbaijan, Georgia and Armenia.

Stock Plzeň, the largest Czech domestic spirits producer, has trebled sales of vodka in the Czech Republic between 2004 and 2009, although wine is rapidly gaining favour in that nation. Its Božkov Vodka has become the top-selling vodka in the retail market, gaining an over 13 per cent market share in the spirits segment and hence overtaking its main rival, the Hanácká Vodka brand. Božkov Vodka is at the top position in restaurants and bars, with a 25 per cent share in vodka sales, followed by brands such as Finlandia (22 per cent) and Vodka Amundsen, also from Stock Plzeň's products, with an over 11 per cent share. Besides its own vodkas, Stock Plzeň also distributes the Finnish Koskenkorva Vodka in the Czech Republic and Slovakia.

Another Czech domestic product is Symphony Vodka, first produced in the eighteenth century. According to its advertising, it has a long and rich tradition, and 'it conjures up images of the great performers who are connected with the Czech Republic, as well as those master composers who were creating their beautiful symphonies at the time'. Consumers of Cannabis Vodka might hear another kind of music. 'Trendy, original, wild, popular and quickly spreading worldwide, this Czech speciality is conquering the nightlife throughout city bars, clubs and discos all around the planet', the distillers proclaim. Their product contains *Cannabis sativa L.* seeds of the Beniko species and can be bought legally in all countries with the exception of Australia. It took a year of government scrutiny before officials in the UK gave the sale of Cannabis Vodka the green light. Some are predicting that since it might be sold in supermarkets, it could replace alcopops in sales to the youth market. Russian officials also found difficulty with Yukos in 2004 when it put its Hemp Vodka on the market, but it was

Koshenkorva Vodka. As one of the world's greatest per capita consumers of vodka, Finland naturally produces its own varieties. This exported brand, made from barley, has sold over a billion bottles since production began in 1953.

also finally approved for Russian consumers. Germany produces Green Hemp Vodka, which consists of only 4 per cent alcohol. Alaska Distillery produces Hemp Purgatory Vodka.

In Brazil the consumption of vodka increased by 30.5 per cent in the period between 2001 and 2003, reaching 3.5 million cases per year. In 2004 alone, the British Allied Domecq Company invested 2.5 million US dollars to launch in Brazil – in partnership with the French Remy Cointreau – the Bols Vodka brand. Diageo considers Brazil to be a target market for vodka. Sales in Brazil are forecast to increase to 7.3 million cases by 2014, when only 3.5 million cases were sold in 2003. With the World Cup football (soccer) competition to be held in Brazil in 2014 and the Olympics in 2016, sales might well spike higher.

Cachaça is Brazil's most common distilled alcoholic beverage. Like rum, it is made from sugarcane. Caipirinha, Brazil's traditional cocktail, consists of crushed ice, cachaça, sugar and fresh lime juice. However, just as vodka has substantially displaced gin in Martinis, so vodka is displacing Brazilian cachaça. The new popular cocktail is called *Caipivodka*. Brazilians apparently like vodka so much that they are buying Orloff Gas, a sparkling carbonated vodka drink with only 15 per cent alcoholic content.

HEMP SEED
purgatory
VODKA
35% ALCOHOL BY VOLUME
(70 PROOF) 750 ML

Hemp Purgatory Vodka. A new product from Alaska Distillery, this hemp-flavoured vodka is an example of the creative infusions that deviate from the more traditional fruit and herb flavours.

In South Africa domestic vodka, labelled predictably with a Russian name, Count Pushkin, has teamed up with a local airline, 1time, whose planes are painted in the Count Pushkin colours and whose interior overhead bins advertise the drink. Winners of an essay competition held in May 2009, extolling the beverage, won a hamper replete with playing cards, wallets and, of course, Count Pushkin Vodka.

In short, emerging markets present vodka distilleries opportunities to sell their premium vodkas, appealing particularly to new urban entrepreneurs and upwardly mobile young populations that are exposed to intense advertising campaigns. According to a 2008 Nielsen survey of international alcoholic beverage trends, vodka is the largest of the spirits categories and has become a truly international choice.

Since vodka is a neutral spirit, it lends itself to blending with flavours and fortifying other beverages. The US represents

Count Pushkin Vodka. This premium South African brand cross-promotes its product with 1time Airlines.

the fastest growing market for flavoured vodkas, which constitute 30 per cent of all vodka sales. Flavoured vodka is beginning to take off in Europe and the rest of the world as well. Flowers, fruits, and seeds of many grasses, herbs, shrubs and trees, both native and imported from far lands, are used to make vodka all over the world. Sweden produces 40 or more different vodkas with various herbs. For example, the American rye Square One Botanical Vodka is infused with a blend of eight organic botanicals – pear, rose, chamomile, lemon verbena, lavender, rosemary, coriander and orange peel. They also offer a basil-infused vodka. Even more laden with flowers, the Swedish wheat Pinky Vodka is hand-blended with violets, rose petals and ten other botanicals, and advertised as 'kissed with the delicate fragrance of a midnight garden'. These botanical drinks are balanced with heartier drinks such as a bacon-flavoured vodka. Bakon Vodka, created by three friends in Seattle, isn't made with real bacon but with various chemicals. Promoted as vegan and gluten-free it is more smoky and strongly flavoured than real bacon infusions. One home producer has flavoured his own vodka with bacon. He suggests making a Martini with it or mixing bacon vodka with pickle juice and date syrup to make a cordial, or even spraying the beverage on salads, adding it to stews or other meat dishes. Other culinary flavours include smoked salmon, ham and cheese, *foie gras* and even lamb. If you would like some seasoning for your meaty vodkas, you could chase them down with horseradish vodka. And of course it can work the other way around – one enterprising bar owner in New York served a Thanksgiving Day meal of soused turkey. It was reportedly the idea of his Irish mother. He infused the bird for three days with 100-proof vodka flavoured with peach, raspberry, cherry and apple. The fowl meal included gravy doused with vodka, cranberry sauce, sweet potatoes and a cab ride to any destination in Manhattan. This meal has greatly changed since the days of the Pilgrims, who first celebrated Thanksgiving in America.

Vegetables and other types of food mixed with vodka are also served in some bars, such as The Russian Vodka Room in New York, which serves a $25 'cavitini', a cocktail based on vodka, with caviar sitting atop a slice of cucumber floating in the glass. Hangar One vodka offers vodka flavoured either with chipotle or wasabi. Perhaps even more bizarre is the bubblegum-flavoured Three O Bubble vodka made by Three Olives and promoted by reality-TV stars Kim and Khloe Kardashian. Is this flavour designed to appeal to the child within us?

In 1994 Finland's Finlandia was one of the first among premium brands to introduce fruit fusions: Cranberry and

Bakon Vodka, an American potato vodka with artificial bacon flavouring. It is one of a wide variety of new vodkas designed to blend with other ingredients and spirits to create flavourful cocktails.

Smoked Salmon Vodka. Alaska Distillery has taken advantage of its abundant access to salmon to produce this creative variety. Virtually any meat, fish, herb or spice can lend itself to creative vodka distillers, while appealing to adventurous consumers.

then Lime, Mango, Redberry, Grapefruit and Tangerine. In 1996 Stolichnaya expanded its flavour portfolio, releasing six new ones into global markets. In the past decade this portfolio has grown and currently offers eight distinctly naturally flavoured vodkas: Stoli Razberi, Stoli Oranj, Stoli Vanil, Stoli Peachik, Stoli Cranberi, Stoli Citros, Stoli Strasberi and, as of May 2006, Stoli Blueberi. California's Skyy Vodka's flavours include pineapple, cherry, grape, melon, raspberry, citrus, passionfruit, vanilla and orange. Fresh fruit infusions appeal to consumers looking for natural and fresh foods, who can imagine (or convince themselves) that such drinks are healthy, especially when the fruit is displayed on the glass bottle's label. Another attraction of infusions, according to a spokesperson, is that 'people have been trading down from the ultra-luxury vodkas' to more affordable luxury infused products from a known brand. Smirnoff offers flavoured vodka, which it calls 'twists', such as Citrus, Cranberry, Orange, Apple, Raspberry, Black Cherry and Lime. Permafrost, besides its straight vodka, offers lychee fruit flavouring. The Dutch super-premium Van Gogh Vodka boasts nineteen vodka infusions. California's Charbay Vodka advertises the following fruit flavours: Blood Orange, Meyer Lemon, Red Raspberry and Pomegranate. Some bars make their own infusions with fruits, vegetables or herbs. They place unflavoured vodka in large jars, let the infusions soak for about five days, remove the flavouring agents, filter, and serve a freshly infused vodka, which many claim has a stronger, fresher flavour than commercial vodkas.

Some new vodkas, however, eliminate infusions or flavouring with fruit and make the vodka directly from the fruit itself. In October 2009 a new vodka appeared in Miami clubs, 4 Orange Vodka, made from Parson Brown, Temple, Valencia and Hamlin oranges (the juice of twenty in 750 ml) grown in Florida. A Herefordshire firm came out in 2009 with a new vodka distilled from organic English cider apples, Naked Chase, so named because nothing else is added to this 42 per cent vodka.

Moving away from fruit flavours, Three Olives features the bold taste of Triple Shot Espresso, Root Beer and Tomato. Spain's Spiritual Vodka contains the 'sweetest caramel'. Another sweet vodka cocktail is the invention of Todd Thatcher, a well-known American 'mixologist', who offers what he calls a 'McGriddle', which tastes like a maple-flavoured pancake from McDonald's. He mixes bacon-infused vodka with cream, maple syrup, a whole egg and confectioner's sugar. A consumer pronounced it as very sweet and good as a dessert drink. Another sweet vodka drink might perhaps appeal only to Americans accustomed to eating candy-corn on Halloween. The vodka is made by simply soaking the candy in a bottle with vodka for several hours, and perhaps adding another liqueur to the mixture, to provide a sweet and familiar-tasting cocktail. Modern Spirits has produced Pumpkin Pie Vodka

Naked Chase vodka. Made from organically grown cider apples, this English vodka might not appeal to vodka traditionalists, but to its fans it is delectable.

made with puréed pumpkin and spices, another sweet treat for the fall season. For the British taste, there is Chase Marmalade Vodka. Infusing vodka into ice cream, not the other way around, on the other hand, produces vodka ice cream. It does not appear to be marketed widely as yet, but homemade varieties can be produced. Israeli bakers have devised another delectable way for adults to consume vodka by baking Hanukkah donuts (*sufganiya*) infused with jam and Horitza Vodka, equivalent to the alcoholic content of a can of beer.

For centuries vodka has been drunk plain or infused. While many infused vodkas are on the market, some people

Pinnacle Whipped Cream Vodka. This American vodka may be drunk neat by those with a sweet tooth, but it is primarily designed to be mixed with liqueurs or other vodkas flavoured with chocolate or coffee, to produce a sweet cocktail. It is an example of the expanding market for exotic vodka flavours favoured by younger drinkers.

enjoy infusing their own vodka as a creative enterprise, some-times involving exercise. One English imbiber recommends walking about, exploiting hedgerows with elderflowers or sloes, gardens with plums, or fields with strawberries, black-berries, blueberries and raspberries. Gardens also yield rhubarb for infusion and virtually any herb. Anyone can infuse plain vodka with vanilla beans. Plain vodka is also the main ingre-dient for cocktails including the vodka Martini. There are chocolate drinks with vodka, even mixing chocolate with bacon-flavoured vodka, and the so-called zulu, a lethal-sounding drink featuring vodka, gin, rum and tequila, is served in a tall glass with sparkling blood-orange juice. In short, if you put your mind to it, you can put almost anything in vodka and you can combine vodka with nearly any other liquor or juice, or as noted with infusions of herbs, fruit, meat, vegetables or sweets, even tossing in a reptile or two. Vicious Vodka, containing caffeine, boasts of having made its bottle more 'vampirish', suggesting bloodthirsty savagery by frosting it and labelling it in black and red. Either the British Blavod Vodka, black in colour because it is made with catechu, an extract found in *Uncaria gambir* trees of Asia, or Vampyre Vodka could be the perfect drink for Halloween.

Some flavoured vodkas are evidently designed to appeal to younger drinkers as well as to adults. Accustomed to sugary soft drinks and highly sweetened beverages, young people on the cusp of coming of legal age to drink alcohol, gravitate to sweet, fruity and rum-flavoured vodka. Youth in Europe and the USA enjoy 'alcopops', that is, flavoured alcohol drinks in

Chase Marmalade Vodka. Infused with Seville oranges, this new vodka reflects the growing variety of fruit-flavoured vodkas.

cans, which are seemingly innocuous but sometimes produce over time a taste for sweet alcohol. Typically, alcopops (a name not recognized by the spirits industry) consist of un-hopped beer from which much of the malt and alcohol is removed but to which vodka or grain alcohol, sugar, colouring and flavouring are added. In the USA these drinks, classified as beer, are sold legally even in places that do not have liquor licences.

Health experts in Italy cite alcopops as one of the reasons for a sharp increase in binge drinking among its youth, because many young consumers perceive alcopops as non-alcoholic. Since the late 1990s Smirnoff has produced a citrus-flavoured malt beverage called Smirnoff Ice which is distributed in the USA and the UK and promoted by ads showing trendy young dancers in odd places and situations. Freaky Ice produces what is claimed to be the only alcoholic ice lolly (popsicle) in the world: 4.6 per cent frozen vodka flavoured with lemon, cherry or passion fruit in a squeezy tube. Originally a Dutch product, it is now made in New York but is banned there as well as in several other states and in New Zealand, Australia, Spain, England and Sweden, because of its obvious similarity to children's ice lollies.

Opponents to the distribution of alcopops or other ready-to-drink alcoholic beverages, usually carbonated, which appeal to youth argue that these drinks, easily mixed and easily disguised, are 'gateways' to later consumption of vodka. It is feared that young people move from these pre-mixes of lower alcoholic content to vodka and by simply adding cranberry or other juices to suit their sweeter tastes, move up the ladder to much stronger beverages. Invers House Distillers at one time distributed, but then discontinued, a carbonated, pre-mixed blend of vodka, taurine and caffeine, flavoured with raspberry and blackcurrant, called Wee Beastie. Fruit-flavoured malt beverages with 9 to 11 per cent alcohol by volume and

Vampyre Vodka. Exploiting the current interest in vampires, this vodka comes in both a clear and a red version. The latter is especially suitable for Halloween parties and is another example of a niche vodka product.

an undisclosed amount of caffeine and other legal stimulants with names such as Evil Eye, Max Fury, Wide Eye, Joose and Slingshot Party Gel usually target college students.

An American study showed that 24 per cent of college students had mixed alcohol with caffeinated beverages within the previous month. A Dutch super-premium vodka, V2, is infused with caffeine and taurine, the essential amino acid found in Red Bull and other energy drinks. Another Dutch wheat vodka, P.I.N.K., contains a unique caffeine and guarana (a potent stimulant) formula for those who want to drink and yet dance the night away. The American potato energy vodka Zygo is infused with flavours as well as with four energy ingredients: guarana, yerba mate, taurine and d-ribose. ViaGuará

Vodka, first produced in Poland, is now available in the USA. It contains guarana and a flavour of ginger. The impression among some young people is that energy vodka raises the metabolism (and hence causes weight loss) and that it can also serve as an aphrodisiac. Some health experts are calling for labels to state the exact amount of caffeine contained in drinks. The US Food and Drug Administration is asking some 27 manufacturers of vodka with caffeine to prove that their products are safe since a task force of state attorneys allege that such drinks lead to an increase in drink-driving, sexual assault and other destructive behaviour as well as possible heart rhythm problems.

II
Vodka's Future

Vodka has truly become an international spirit thanks to its neutrality, simplicity and versatility. In fact it is the chameleon of the alcohol world. Its popularity among Americans has led Nic's restaurant in Beverly Hills, California, to install a 'Vodbox', a unique patented walk-in freezer where about a dozen heavily wrapped customers choose a small bottle of vodka from among as many as 80 varieties and sit in the cold to consume it. Vodka reportedly accounts for 75 per cent of all spirits sold in downtown San Diego, California. As one vodka admirer writes, 'Vodka still rules the world of clear spirits, probably because it is so relatively easy to make and because it can be made from virtually any organic matter.' One might add that it can also be transformed into virtually any kind of drink, allowing the imbiber not only to experience the effects of alcohol but also to project an image of himself while doing so.

A University of St Petersburg professor, Evgeny Moskalev, recently perfected a technique for converting liquid, including vodka, into a powder. Packaging liquids as powders saves space, and bottling. It is also extremely convenient for anyone who would like to have a drink in powdered form, in a capsule. Since the powder tastes like wax, the best use for it appears to be in baking, where the sweetness can mask the flavour. While some might want to pop a capsule from their pockets into their mouths to experience the effects of alcohol, the inventor admits he prefers to drink vodka the old-fashioned way.

Other scientists are inventing ways of purifying vodka. Many drinkers particularly appreciate that vodka is low in fusel oils and impurities, which allegedly can reduce hangovers. In 2009 *R&D Magazine* named Dr Hans van Leeuwen, Vlasta Klima Balloun Professor of Environmental and Biological Engineering at Iowa State University, Innovator of the Year, for his innovations in purifying alcohol and other industrial refinements. His purification process uses ozone and activated carbon to reduce unwanted substances in alcohol, eliminating undesirable tastes and odours, making the product much more mellow. The technique, which supplements typical multi-distillation processes, is now being used to launch Leeuwenoff, the world's purest vodka – and this

Vodbox. This patented invention of Nic's Bar and Restaurant in Beverly Hills, California, is designed to give the customer a total vodka immersion experience in a simulated icebox, although fur coats are advised.

can be proved by van Leeuwen and his colleagues Jacek A. Koziel and Lingshuang Cai.

There is also some medical evidence that moderate use of vodka can even be healthful. A trial in the Netherlands is seeking to discover if a daily shot of vodka can prevent inflammation and congestion in the arteries, thus affording possible protection against diabetes and heart disease. Romanian doctors are also experimenting with daily 'doses' of 30 grams of vodka to treat heart patients in order to save money.

In a fast-paced world, speed is of the essence in producing vodka. The present 'Vodka Age' has shoved gin aside; four times more vodka is consumed than gin. Clearly the taste for vodka has been globalized partly because of its relative ease of production, its massive promotion, its potential for creativity, and versatility. The ceaseless tinkering with infusions and flavours prompted Sean Harrison, a distiller of Plymouth Gin, to quip that pretty soon vodka makers will invent gin. Perhaps this was no joke – after all the Dutch Van Gogh Vodka is producing an absinthe-flavoured vodka!

Indeed, according to a report dated 18 August 2009 vodka is the fastest growing segment of the alcohol industry, reaching total global sales of nearly 513 million cases in 2008, or over three billion litres annually, a figure that shows that the quantity sold has doubled over the past twenty years. Vodka alone now accounts for 18 per cent of world spirit consumption, and 29 per cent of all spirits sales in the USA, impressive figures when one considers that nearly every country has its own traditional kinds of spirits besides vodka. Much of this growth has come in the 'vodka belt' countries of Russia and Poland where our story began. In periods of economic depression vodka consumption does not appear to diminish, although choices shift from premium brands such as Grey Goose, Absolut and Stolichnaya to lower priced brands such as Skyy, Svedka and Sobieski. Diageo, the British spirits company and the world's largest, holds an advantageous position because it owns vodka brands in all price ranges.

Wine, unlike vodka, is defined by its *terroir*, that is, its earthy place, its local identity, its traditional fermentation, its history and its unique microclimate that are needed to produce the same distinctive aroma, flavour and taste year after year and decade after decade. *Terroir* proclaims the product to be Burgundy or Chianti. By definition, a *terroir* wine does not travel until it has been bottled. Even other spirits are identified with specific countries that claim the trademark so that 'Scotch Whisky' can only be produced in Scotland, 'Cognac' and 'Champagne' in France, 'Russian Vodka' in Russia, and 'Bourbon' in the USA. Vodka, on the other hand, has vague roots, yet a distinguished tradition in Poland and Russia, but it is international by nature since it can be replicated anywhere if the same ingredients and the same distillation process are adopted. The entire method of producing vodka wrings its place of origin out of it, reducing it to anonymous alcohol. No one could ever detect its birthplace were it not for the advertising accompanying it. No one would be able to state upon tasting a particular vodka that the potatoes at its base were from Poland, Maine, Ukraine, Idaho or Germany. Nor could one tell if the water used to dilute the alcohol was Oregon river water, water from a New Zealand aquifer, or an Icelandic iceberg. Nor by taste can the filter be identified as sand, quartz, diamond, charcoal or stainless steel mesh. Yet a few distillers retain the notion of *terroir*, arguing that the soil and the raw material do make a difference in determining the quality of vodka.

Vodka, the mysterious drink, can keep its provenance, like its history, secret. Flavours added either by distiller or consumer distinguish the drink by taste, although the nature of

Jazz Vodka.
A Polish Sobieski
product, the
unusual trumpet
shape is meant
to attract music
lovers and bottle
collectors, not
to mention
the attention
of average
consumers.

the mash, as well as the distillation and filtering process, can alter the taste and smoothness of the product. In short, with vodka, geography is not destiny, although it appears that vodka is destined to become global. Vodka had the potential to be globalized even before the concept of globalization arose. With the mobility of populations, the ease of communication, the creation of international infrastructures allowing for foreign ownership and investment, an international demand for the product – in part created by advertisements – and the relative ease of acquiring the know-how for its distillation, vagabond vodka is the ultimate globetrotter. All over the world some people will drink vodka with joy in homage to Bacchus. Others will drink it in homage to Malthus, serving as a check on the world's population.

So what is vodka? Vodka, as it turns out, is something greater than the sum of its own contradictions. What other drink has such a long and rich history, while remaining quintessentially modern? What other drink can be made practically anywhere with anything that grows and still be so Russian and Polish? What other drink is found at so many of life's celebrations, yet brings to life so much sorrow? There is no universal definition of vodka. Instead vodka serves as a prism through which each person may view his or her own life and times. When the great Catalan artist Pablo Picasso was asked what he thought were the most notable features of post-war France, he replied, 'Brigitte Bardot, modern jazz and Polish vodka.'

Recipes

Penne with Vodka Sauce and Sausage

1 lb (450 g) uncooked penne pasta
¼ cup (55 ml) extra virgin olive oil
4 cloves garlic, minced
½ teaspoon crushed red pepper flakes
28 oz (830 g) can of crushed tomatoes
½ teaspoon salt
½ cup (110 ml) vodka
½ cup (110 ml) double (heavy) whipping cream
¼ cup (4 tablespoons) chopped fresh parsley or basil for garnish
1 pound (450 g) sweet Italian sausage taken out of casing and crumbled
freshly grated Parmigiano Reggiano, for garnish

In a large frying pan, heat the oil over a moderate heat. Remove the casings from the sausages and add to the pan. Cook, breaking up the meat, until brown. Add garlic and red pepper and cook, stirring until the garlic is golden brown. Add the tomatoes and the salt, and bring to the boil. Reduce the heat and simmer for 15 minutes. Add the vodka and the cream and bring to the boil. Reduce the heat to low for 3–4 minutes.

While the sauce is simmering, bring a large pot of lightly salted water to the boil. Add the pasta and cook for 8–10 minutes or until al dente. Toss the sauce with the pasta to coat evenly and transfer to a pasta bowl for serving. Top with cheese and parsley or basil and serve.

Serves 6

Pasta with Salmon in Vodka Lemon Dill Cream Sauce

4 shallots (about 1 cup), finely chopped
1 tablespoon olive oil
2½ cups (560 ml) reduced-sodium chicken stock (broth)
1 cup (225 ml) double (heavy) cream
½ cup (110 ml) vodka
¼ teaspoon salt
½ cup (4 tablespoons) chopped fresh dill
1½ teaspoons finely grated lemon zest
2 tablespoons fresh lemon juice
¼ teaspoon coarsely ground black pepper
2 cups (about 1 lb / 450 g) flaked baked, poached or broiled salmon
10 oz (280 g) gemelli or campanelle pasta

Sauté the shallots in oil in a heavy saucepan over a moderate heat until softened (about 6 minutes). Add the stock, cream and vodka, and boil gently until the sauce is reduced to 2 cups (about 1 hour). Remove from the heat and stir in the lemon zest and juice, and pepper. Set aside ½ cup of sauce. Add the salmon to the saucepan and warm over a low heat for 2–3 minutes. Cook pasta in a large pot of boiling salted water until al dente (about 10 minutes). Drain the pasta in a colander. Return the pasta to the pot, and toss with the reserved sauce. Toss with the chopped dill. Serve immediately with fish and sauce spooned over the top.

Serves 4

Seared Scallops with Lemon and Vodka

1 lb (450 g) sea scallops
1 tablespoon plus 1 teaspoon olive oil
⅔ cup (135 ml) vodka
2 tablespoons double (heavy) cream
1 tablespoon freshly squeezed lemon juice
1 teaspoon finely grated lemon zest
2 tablespoons fresh tarragon leaves, chopped

Pat the scallops dry with paper towel, rub with 1 teaspoon of the olive oil, and season with salt and freshly ground black pepper. Heat the remaining oil in a large frying pan over a high heat. When the oil shimmers, add the scallops and cook on each side until golden brown (about 5 minutes in total). Transfer to a plate and set aside.

Remove the pan from the heat and carefully add the vodka, scraping up any browned bits from the bottom of the pan and stirring to incorporate into the sauce. Return the pan to a medium-low heat and add the cream, lemon juice and lemon zest; stir to combine. Return the scallops and any accumulated juices to the pan and cook until heated through (about 2 minutes). Stir in the tarragon. The dish can be accompanied with rice or crusty bread to soak up the sauce.

Serves 2

Jelly (Jello) Shots

These are colourful (and strong) additions to parties, not to be gulped in succession.

Lemon, lime or orange-flavoured jelly (jello) combines nicely with matching flavoured vodkas.

To make extra firm shots, add a little unflavoured gelatine to the jelly.

Unflavoured gelatine can be used instead of jelly, but the colours will not be as vivid. If unflavoured gelatine such as Knox is used, add a bit of sugar. Add food colouring as desired.

Experiment with different as well as matching flavours of vodka with the gelatine, using boiling juice, such as cranberry juice, instead of water.

This recipe allows for your creativity.

1 packet of powdered jelly (jello)
6 oz (180 ml) chilled vodka
6 oz (180 ml) boiling water

Bring more than 1 cup (225 ml) of water to a boil. (You'll need exactly 1 cup of boiling water, so put a little more than that in the pot or kettle, since some will evaporate.) Measure out the boiling water and mix it with the powdered jelly. Stir constantly until the powder is completely dissolved.

Stir in the chilled vodka. Pour the mixture into small paper cups or shot glasses. Place the shots on a tray in the refrigerator (not the freezer). Chill until firm (approximately 2–4 hours). Allow to set completely. Refrigerate until served.
Serves 8

Vodka Martini

This drink, made famous by James Bond movies, remains a favourite. It is so simple to make.

1–2 oz (60 ml) vodka according to desired strength
dash of dry vermouth
twist of lemon peel, or one green olive, or one cocktail onion
as garnish

Pour the vodka over ice in a large glass. Add the vermouth and stir well. Strain into a Martini glass. Garnish with lemon peel, an olive or a small pickled onion.

Bloody Mary

Invented supposedly in 1921 in Harry's Bar in Venice, this drink is often served at brunches or even as a remedy for hangovers. A wide variety of spices and garnishes are used for this drink. But the basics are the following:

2 oz (60 ml) vodka*
tomato juice
dash of Worcestershire sauce
dash of Tabasco sauce
juice of half a lemon
pinch of cayenne pepper
pinch of celery salt
for garnish: celery stalk with leaves, carrot stick, wedge of lemon, or dill pickle spear

Put ice in a tall highball glass. Add dashes of Worcestershire sauce, Tabasco sauce, lemon juice, celery salt and cayenne pepper to the glass. Pour in the vodka. Fill the glass with tomato juice. Stir gently. Garnish with a celery stalk, carrot stick, lemon wedge or pickle spear.

*Instead of unflavoured vodka, you can use pepper vodka, horseradish vodka, bacon or dill-flavoured vodka to spice up the cocktail.

Moscow Mule

Invented in 1941 in Los Angeles, California, by two businessmen, one with too much vodka on his hands and the other with too much ginger beer, this drink became controversial during the Cold War.

2 oz (60 ml) vodka
1 oz (30 ml) lime juice

1 teaspoon sugar syrup
ginger beer
sprig of fresh mint

Fill a copper mug or tumbler half full with crushed ice, pour in the vodka and lime juice. Fill the rest of the mug with ginger beer. Stir. Garnish with the lime wedge and sprig of mint.

Black Russian

Appearing first in 1949, this became popular in the 1980s. This drink is to be sipped.

2 oz (60 ml) vodka
1 oz (30 ml) coffee liqueur

Pour some crushed ice into a tumbler, add liquids. Stir.

White Russian

Follow the instructions for a Black Russian, but top with cream, half-milk and half-cream, or whole milk.

Vodka Mojito

The name of this drink is of uncertain origin, perhaps meaning 'blend' or perhaps 'little soul'. The drink itself, originally made with rum, appeared in Cuba in the late 1920s.

2 oz (60 ml) vodka
3 sprigs fresh mint
2 tablespoons sugar
2 tablespoons fresh lime juice
3 tablespoons fresh lemon juice

soda water
lemon or lime twist for garnish

Muddle the mint, sugar and citrus juices in a tall glass. Nearly fill the glass with ice, add the vodka, and top with chilled soda water. Garnish with a lemon or lime twist.

Japanese Slipper (with green Midori)

This green drink looks refreshing but the slipper can give a good kick too.

1½ oz (45 ml) vodka
1 oz (30 ml) Midori
1 oz (30 ml) Cointreau
1 oz (30 ml) fresh lime juice
lime slice for garnish
6 ice cubes, crushed

Place the crushed ice into a cocktail shaker and add liquids. Shake well and strain into Martini glasses. Add the lime garnish and serve.

Harvey Wallbanger (with Galliano)

This is a popular party drink said to have been invented by a bartender in 1952 and named for a surfer and patron of a Hollywood bar.

1½ oz (45 ml) vodka
½ oz (15 ml) Galliano
3 oz (90 ml) fresh orange juice
orange slice for garnish

Stir the vodka and orange juice with ice in a tall highball glass. Float the Galliano on top. Garnish with the orange slice and serve.

Screwdriver

The earliest written reference to the Screwdriver is from the 24 October 1949 issue of *Time* magazine. Supposedly, American petroleum engineers in Saudi Arabia – where alcohol is forbidden – secretly added vodka to orange juice and stirred the drink with their screwdrivers.

2 oz (60 ml) vodka
6 oz (120 ml) fresh orange juice

Add the vodka to an ice-filled glass and top with orange juice.

Double Espresso

This easy-to-make drink is a coffee lovers' delight.

crushed ice
2 oz (30 ml) espresso coffee
2 oz (30 ml) coffee-flavoured vodka
1 teaspoon caster (superfine) sugar

Mix all the ingredients together with ice in a cocktail shaker. Shake well. Strain into small glasses.

Vodka Around the World

Below is a sampling of what awaits you if you are on the road or touring the world. Bottoms up!

Australia

CoranBong Vodka (grapes, ten times distilled)
DOT AU **Vodka** (Australian sugar cane, three times distilled, filtered through ancient elements)
Downunder Vodka (molasses of Australian sugar cane, three times distilled in a copper column)

Austria

Monopolowa Vodka (potato, three times distilled)
Oval Vodka (wheat, three times distilled)

Azerbaijan

Xan Vodka (grain, three times filtered)

Belarus

Berezovaya Birch Vodka (grain and birch syrup)
Kryshtal Etalon Vodka (wheat and rye, four times distilled, filtered once)
Minskaya Kristall Vodka (wheat and rye, four times distilled, filtered several times)

Belgium

Black Queen Vodka (grain and herbs, four times distilled)
Hertenkamp Vodka (grain, filtered through active carbon)
Van Hoo Vodka (grain, four times distilled, charcoal filtered)

Bulgaria

Balkan Vodka (grain, three times distilled)

Canada

Alberta Pure Vodka (prairie grains, three times distilled, filtered)
Crystal Head Vodka (grains, four times distilled, three times filtered through charcoal and Herkimer diamond crystals)
Iceberg Vodka (sweetcorn, three times distilled, iceberg water)
Inferno Pepper Vodka (rye, four times distilled, charcoal filtered)
Pearl Vodka (wheat, five times distilled, six times filtered)
Polar Ice Vodka (grains, four times distilled, three times filtered)
Schramm Vodka (organic potato, copper pot distilled, charcoal filtered)
Signature Vodka (grains, herbs, five times distilled, spring water)

China

Shanghai White Vodka (grain, four times distilled)

Croatia

Akvinta Vodka (organic Italian wheat, three times distilled, five times filtered with charcoal, marble, gold, silver and platinum)

Czech Republic

Božkov Vodka (molasses, three times filtered through cellulose)
Symphony Vodka (potato, two times coal filtered)

Denmark

Danzka Vodka (wholewheat, four times distilled, three times filtered)
Fris Vodka (wheat, freeze distilled)

England

Blavod Black Vodka (molasses, three times distilled, two times filtered)
Chase Vodka (potato, copper pot five times distilled, charcoal filtered)
Chekov Imperial Vodka (grain, three times distilled)
Cristalnaya Vodka (grains and botanicals, three times distilled)
Red Square Vodka (grain, three times distilled, carbon filtered)
Tanqueray Sterling Vodka (grain, high proof distillation)

Three Olives Vodka (wheat, four times distilled, four times filtered)

Vampyre Red Vodka (wheat, three times distilled, filtered through ten micron filters)

Estonia

Stön Vodka (wheat, four times distilled, limestone filtered)

The Tall Blond Vodka (variety of grains, triple distilled)

Türi Vodka (rye, four times distilled, charcoal filtered)

Viru Valge Vodka (grain)

Finland

Finlandia Vodka (barley, continuous multi-pressure distillation)

Koskenkorva Vodka (barley, distilled over 250 times)

France

Cîroc Vodka (grape, five times distilled)

Dragon Bleu Vodka (wheat, barley, rye, once micro distilled)

Grey Goose Vodka (wheat, five-step-copper-pot distilled, lime-stone-filtered water)

Idôl Vodka (Chardonnay and Pinot Noir grapes, seven times distilled, five times filtered)

Jean-Marc xo Vodka (four varieties of wheat, nine times copper pot distilled, Limousin oak charcoal filtered)

Perfect *1864* Vodka (wheat, five times distilled, lightly filtered through cotton membrane)

Quay Vodka (wheat and rye, five times distilled, four times filtered)

Georgia

Eristoff Vodka (grain, three times distilled, charcoal filtered)

Germany

Gorbatschow Vodka (grain, three times cold filtered, two times charcoal filtered)
Vallure Vodka (multi-distilled, three times gold filtered)

Greenland

Siku Glacial Ice Vodka (grain, five times distilled, glacier ice)

Iceland

Reyka Vodka (wheat and barley, distillery operated by geothermal heat, volcanic rock filtered)

India

Romanoff Vodka (mixed grains, three times distilled, three times filtered)
White Mischief Vodka (mixed grains, three times distilled, carbon filtered)

Ireland

Boru Vodka (barley, five times distilled, oak charcoal filtered)
Huzzar Vodka (grain, three times distilled, silver birch charcoal filtered)

Italy

due' Vodka (grain and grape, four times distilled using four columns)
Mezzaluna Vodka (100 per cent semolina grain, three times distilled, four times filtered)
Roberto Cavalli Vodka (grain, five times distilled, filtered through Carrara marble chips)

Kazakhstan

Snow Queen Vodka (organic wheat, five times distilled, birch charcoal filtered)

Latvia

Dannoff Vodka (winter wheat, four times distilled, active charcoal filtered)

Lithuania

Lithuania Original Vodka (grain, three times distilled, sand, quartz, activated birch charcoal filtered)
Ozone Vodka (grain, multi-state filtered)
Stumbras Vodka (grains, silver filtered)

Mexico

Villa Lobos Vodka (corn, wheat and barley, five times distilled)

Moldova

Exclusive Vodka (winter wheat, distilled five times)
Firestarter Vodka (winter wheat, five times distilled, filtered)

Mongolia

Chinggis Vodka (wheat, eight times distilled, filtered through quartz sand and silver birch activated carbon)
Grandkhaan Vodka (wheat, year-long distillation, 29 times filtered)

Netherlands

Bols Vodka (grain, four times distilled, filtered through copper-coal)
Bong Spirit Vodka (wheat, six times distilled, four times charcoal filtered)
Cardinal Vodka (wheat, three times step-by-step distillation)
Effen Vodka (premium wheat, continuous rectification distillation, peat filtered)
Ketel One Vodka (wheat, copper pot distillation family secret since 1691, charcoal filtered)
Royalty Vodka (wheat, four times distilled, activated carbon five times filtered)
Sex II IV VII VI III VI V Vodka (grains, four column distillation, three times filtered)
Ursus Vodka (grain, three times distilled)
Vincent Van Gogh Vodka (wheat, corn and barley, three times distilled)
Vox Vodka (wheat, five times distilled)

New Zealand

26000 **Vodka** (grain, three times charcoal filtered, 26,000-year-old underground water)
42 **Below Vodka** (rye, five times distilled, charcoal filtered)

Norway

Vikingfjord Vodka (potato, five times distilled, charcoal filtered)

Poland

Belvedere Vodka (rye, four times distilled in copper column stills, three times charcoal filtered)
Chopin Vodka (potato, four times distilled)
Evolution Vodka (rye, five times distilled, filtered through activated carbon)
Jazz Vodka (grain, four times distilled, charcoal filtered)
Krolewska Vodka (rye, four times distilled, filtered)
Luksusowa Vodka (potato, three times distilled, filtered through charcoal and oak chips)
Military Five Vodka (grain, three times distilled)
Original Polish Vodka (rye, six times distilled, three times filtered)
Potocki Vodka (rye, two times distilled, not filtered)
Pravda Vodka (rye, five-step distillation)
Shakespeare Vodka (rye, four times distilled)
Sobieski Vodka (rye, once distilled)
Soplica Vodka (rye, four times distilled, activated charcoal filtered)
Ultimat Vodka (wheat, rye and potato, hydro-selection distillation, ceramic filtered)
U'Luvka Vodka (rye, wheat and barley, three times distilled)
Wyborowa Vodka (rye, three times distilled)
Zubrówka Vodka (rye and bison grass)

Russia

Beluga Vodka (malt spirits, three times distilled, Siberian spring water, honey, oat extract and milk thistle, aged 30 days)
Cristall Vodka (grain, unique distillation process, filtered through quartz crystals and carbon granules)
Flagman Vodka (wheat, three times distilled, filtered)
Imperia Vodka (wheat, eight times distilled, crystal quartz filtered)
Kalashnikov Vodka (grain, water from Lake Ladoga)
Kauffman Vodka (wheat of a single harvest, fourteen times distilled, two times filtered, once through birch coal and once through quartz sand)
Jewel of Russia Vodka (winter wheat and rye, five-step slow filtration through charcoal of peach and apricot stones)
Mamont Vodka (Siberian wheat, five times distilled, filtered three times through birch bark)
Moskovskaya Vodka (rye and wheat, pure glacial water)
Rodnik Vodka (winter wheat, birch wood filtered)
Russian Standard Vodka (winter wheat, four times distilled in 35-metre rectification column, charcoal filtered)
Stolichnaya Vodka (wheat and rye, four times distilled, four times filtered through quartz, activated charcoal and cloth)
Tovaritch Vodka (wheat, five times distilled, three times birch charcoal filtered)
Tsarskaya Vodka (grain, lime tree honey and lime blossoms to flavour)
Zelyonaya Marka Vodka (wheat, platinum and silver filtered)
Zyr Vodka (winter wheat and rye, five times distilled, four times birch tree charcoal filtered)

Scotland

Armadale Vodka (wheat and barley, three times distilled)
Vladivar Vodka (grain, three times distilled, charcoal filtered)

Slovak Republic

Doktor Vodka (two times filtered)
Double Cross Vodka (estate-grown winter wheat, seven times distilled, seven times filtered)
V44 Vodka (wheat, four times distilled, filtered through shungite mineral)

South Africa

Romanoff Vodka (molasses, column still)
Count Pushkin Vodka (five times distilled)

South Korea

Han Vodka (barley and rice)

Sweden

Absolut Vodka (winter wheat, continuous distillation)
Cape North Vodka (French wheat, five times distilled in copper pot still, terracotta filtered)
Cariel Vodka (barley and winter wheat, three times distilled)
DQ Vodka (winter wheat, multiple column continuous distillation)
Karlsson's Gold Vodka (potato, once distilled, unfiltered)
Level Vodka (winter wheat, continuous distillation and pot still)
Svedka Vodka (winter wheat, five times distilled, charcoal filtered)

Switzerland

Xellent Swiss Vodka (rye, distilled three times)

Turkey

Lokka Vodka (grape, distilled five times)

Ukraine

Khortytsa Vodka (wheat, modern distillation process, filtered through crystals)
Nemiroff Vodka and **Nemiroff Honey Pepper Vodka** (wheat, charcoal filtered)

United States

Bee Vodka (honey, three times distilled, copper pot still, copper column)
Black Lab Vodka (grain, water from Cascades Mountains, five times charcoal filtered)
Cirrus Vodka (potato, triple distilled in pot still, filtered)
Cold River Vodka (potato, three times distilled in copper pot)
Death's Door Vodka (hard red winter wheat and malted barley, small batch triple distilled in hybrid pot and column still)
LiV Vodka (potato, copper stills, three times distilled)
Moon Mountain Vodka (corn, copper pot still distillation)
Permafrost Vodka (potato, triple distilled, glacier water)
Popov Vodka (grain, one time distilled, filtered through charcoal)
Rain Organics Vodka (organic white corn, seven times distilled, filtered through activated carbon and diamond dust)
Skyy Vodka (wheat, four times distilled, three times charcoal filtered)
Smirnoff Vodka (grain, three times distilled, ten times charcoal filtered)
Square One Organic Vodka (organic rye, 64-column distillation, filtered once through micro paper)
Tito's Handmade Vodka (corn, six times distilled)
UV Vodka (corn, four times distilled, activated carbon filtered)

v-One Vodka (spelt wheat, five times distilled in Poland)

Vodka *14* (organic corn and rye, four column continuous distillation, activated carbon and crystal filtered)

Vodka *7000* (oats, copper pot distilled, filtered through deep rock aquifers)

Zodiac Vodka (potato, four-column 91-stage distillation process, filtered through Canadian birch charcoal and rock crystal)

Wales

Brecon Five Vodka (wheat and barley, five times distilled)

Bibliography

Christian, David, *Living Water: Vodka and Society on the Eve of Revolution* (Oxford, 1990)

Ermochkine, Nicholas and Peter Iglikowski, *40 Degrees East: An Anatomy of Vodka* (New York, 2003)

Hamilton, Carl, *Absolut: Biography of a Bottle* (London, 2000)

Herlihy, Patricia, *The Alcoholic Empire: Vodka and Politics in Late Imperial Russia* (Oxford, 2002)

—, 'Revenue and Revelry on Tap: The Russian Tavern', *Alcohol, A Social and Cultural History*, ed. Mack Holt (Oxford, 2006)

—, 'Joy of the Rus': Rites and Rituals of Russian Drinking', *Russian Review*, 50 (April 1991), pp. 131–47

Himselstein, Linda, *The King of Vodka: The Story of Pyotr Smirnov and the Upheaval of an Empire* (New York, 2009)

Kerr, W. Park, and Leigh Beisch, *Viva Vodka: Colorful Cocktails With a Kick* (San Francisco, CA, 2006)

Levinson, Charles, *Vodka Cola* (London and New York, 1978)

Lewis, Richard W., *Absolut Book: The Absolut Vodka Advertising Story* (Boston, MA, 1996)

Long, Lucy M., ed., *Culinary Tourism* (Lexington, KY, 2004)

Nicholas, Faith, and Ian Wisniewski, *Classic Vodka* (London, 1997)

Phillips, Laura A., *Bolsheviks and the Bottle: Drink and Worker Culture in St. Petersburg, 1900–1929* (De Kalb, IL, 2000)

Pokhlebkin, Viliam Vasilevich, *A History of Vodka* (London and New York, 1992)

Ruby, Scott, 'A Toast to Vodka and Russia', in *The Art of*

Drinking, ed. Philippa Glanville and Sophie Lee (London, 2007), pp. 126–33

Simpson, Scott, 'History and Mythology of Polish Vodka: 1270–2007', *Food and History,* vol. VIII/I (2010), pp. 121–48

Starling, Boris, *Vodka* (London, 2004)

Transchel, Kate, *Under the Influence: Working-Class Drinking, Temperance, and Cultural Revolution in Russia, 1895–1932* (Pittsburgh, PA, 2006)

Vodka: Invigorating Vodka Cocktails (London, 2007)

Walton, Stuart, *Vodka Classified: A Vodka Lover's Companion* (London, 2009)

White, Stephen, *Russia Goes Dry: Alcohol, State and Society* (Cambridge and New York, 1996)

Websites and Associations

Vodka recipes

www.vodka-club.net

www.drinkswap.com

Vodka reviews

vodkabuzz.com/vodkas

www.russianlife.com

www.vodkabottle.com

Vodka brands

www.onlinevodka.net

www.beverageunderground.com

Russian vodkas

www.russianvodka.com

Dutch vodka

http://vodkayeast.com

Acknowledgements

I raise my *charka* to David, Felix, Gregory and Irene Herlihy for reading the manuscript and for making comments, suggestions and corrections. Gregory Herlihy was invaluable in making the index. Kathleen McBride was indispensable in helping with the images. She and Helen F. Schmierer were my recipe consultants to whom I am most grateful. Helen F. Schmierer and Christopher Herlihy kindly provided me with research material. My discussions with Sarah W. Tracy about vodka and its significance stimulated my thinking, and ultimately, writing of this book. Liuba Shrirar checked my Russian captions. She, Maurice Herlihy and Steven Marks furnished some of the anecdotes recounted in this volume. Linda Himmelstein graciously assisted me with tracking down some vodka companies.

For Polish material I am indebted to the generosity of Scott Simpson, Patrice Dabrowski, and especially to Lukasz Czajka whose website www.czajkus.friko.pl provided several images for this book. I thank Vitaly Komar for his charming Vodkard. Two anonymous collectors granted me permission to reproduce photographs in their possession; to one I say *spasibo*; to the other *merci*.

In friendship and with happy memories I toast all my vodka-drinking companions from Odessa to Moscow and from all over the USA.

Photo Acknowledgements

The author and the publishers wish to express their thanks to the below sources of illustrative material and/or permission to reproduce it:

Anonymous collector: pp. 9, 10, 39, 50, 51, 52; Altia Company, Finland: p. 114; Bakon Vodka Co.: p. 118; Bolshoi Theater: p. 25; © The Trustees of the British Museum, London: p. 8; Roberto Cavalli Vodka Co.: p. 108; Chase Distillery Ltd: pp. 121, 123; Cold River Vodka, Freeport, Maine: p. 15; Corbis: p. 62 (Pascale Le Segretain/ Sygma); Crystal Head Vodka: p. 83; Lukasz Czajka: pp. 28–9, 44, 94, 95; Courtesy of Diageo: pp. 69, 85, 110; Death's Door Spirits: p. 84; Distilleries LLG Alaska Distilleries: pp. 18, 42, 115, 119; Dreamstime: p. 72 (Buddy Mays); DSG-Group s.a.: p. 99; Fire- starter: p. 80; Gersheim Photographic Corpus of Drawings: p. 48; Getty Images: p. 17; Harvard Fine Arts Library, Visual Collection: p. 54; Imperator Ltd: p. 23; Imperial Brands Limited: p. 41; Istock- photo: p. 6 (Mafaldita); Vitaly Komar: p. 60; Michael Leaman: p. 16; Library of Congress, Washington, DC: p. 34; London Island Spirits: p. 100; Marussia Beverages B.V.: p. 75; The New Muscovy Company: p. 33; New York Public Library: p. 57; Nic's Beverly Hills: p. 128; Sobieski: p. 131; SSB Trade LLC: p. 112; Signature Vodka (MASV): p. 21; University of California, San Diego: p. 73; US National Library of Medicine, Bethesda, Maryland: pp. 13, 36, 64; Valentine Distilling Co.: p. 11; Vampyre Vodka Company: p. 125; Vodka Museum, Uglich, Russia: p. 35; Waterdog Spirits, LLC: p. 88; White Mischief: p. 109; White Rock Distilleries: p. 122.

Index

italic numbers refer to illustrations; **bold** to recipes